ECONOMIC SYSTEMS IN ACTION

The United States, the Soviet Union, and the United Kingdom

Economic Systems in Action

THE UNITED STATES, THE SOVIET UNION, *and* THE UNITED KINGDOM

Alfred R. Oxenfeldt

ASSOCIATE PROFESSOR OF ECONOMICS
COLLEGE OF THE CITY OF NEW YORK

ASSOCIATE, BONI, WATKINS, MOUNTEER, & CO., INC., CONSULTING ECONOMISTS

RINEHART & COMPANY, INC.
NEW YORK

Seventh Printing, July 1955

Printed in the United States of America

Designed by Stefan Salter

Library of Congress Catalog Card Number: 52–5611

To the Memory of My Father, Harry Oxenfeldt

He that would seriously set upon the search of truth, ought in the first place to prepare his mind with a love of it. . . . How a man may know whether he be so in earnest, is worth inquiry: and I think there is one unerring mark of it, *viz.* the not entertaining any proposition with greater assurance, than the proofs it is built upon will warrant. Whoever goes beyond this measure of assent, it is plain, receives not truth in the love of it; loves not truth for truth-sake, but for some other by-end.

JOHN LOCKE, *The Dangers of Enthusiasm*

Preface

This book is intended to fill a gap in the literature about economic systems. Most of the available material in this field, much of which is of very high caliber, falls into one of two classes: brief and necessarily superficial discussions or long and comprehensive books. The difficulties in such treatments for the average reader, or for the student who does not wish to specialize but wishes an introduction to the subject, are obvious: the brief study tells him far less than he should know; the detailed one tells him too much and is frequently, in addition, extremely technical. This book is of intermediate size and is generally nontechnical in character. It should therefore suit the needs, and not be beyond the ready comprehension of an intelligent high school graduate who is interested in contemporary problems.

I trust that the book has merits other than its size. It is the only discussion of economic systems, to my knowledge, that is organized around the basic functions that every economic system is expected to perform. About each system is asked: how is what should be produced determined, and does output actually consist of the things that the people most want and need? How are methods of production selected, and how efficiently does each system operate? How are individuals directed into occupations; do most persons get into employments for which they are highly qualified, and do they have an opportunity to develop their full productive capabilities? How is personal income determined, and how equally is it distributed? What factors influence the progressiveness of each economy, and how progressive is it?

This method of organization has at least one possible disadvantage that partly offsets its obvious advantages. Much of the information that is available about economic systems does not bear directly on these questions. As a result, I have been required to raise many questions that I have been unable to answer. This choice seemed preferable to the alternative of organizing the discussion around the material available, for such a course would fail to weigh information according to its relevance to the basic functioning of an economic system.

Every author on controversial subjects doubtless feels that his presentation possesses the special virtue of impartiality. Certainly this book is as unprejudiced as I can make it. Indeed, several persons have told me that I have leaned over backward to be fair to viewpoints I do not share. As I reread the entire book as a whole, I think I find traces of two types of prejudice. First, I probably have been overcritical of all three systems. That is to say, I probably have stressed the limitations of each economy and passed rather quickly over its virtues. This prejudice, if it can be so called, reflects my conviction that a major function of economic science is to discover shortcomings in existing arrangements so that they may be remedied.

Second, I suspect myself of prejudice against widely held conclusions that are either entirely unfounded or inconsistent with most available evidence. I have perhaps been less gentle with unsupported views than some readers would have liked. Here, too, I would submit that a major function of economic science, as of any other science, is to demand that opinion be amply rooted in fact.

Many persons have read sections of this book and by their suggestions have improved it immeasurably. I have received the greatest help from Gertrude E. Oxenfeldt, who, concerning the substance and form of the book, was—as in all matters—both my keenest and most constructive critic. Professor Arthur R. Burns, of Columbia University, gave the entire manuscript a thorough and discerning reading and contributed many helpful suggestions. Professors William N. Leonard, of Penn State, George Halm, of the Fletcher School of Law and Diplomacy, and Henry H. Villard, of the College of the City of New York, commented on the entire manuscript, eliminated errors, and suggested points deserving greater space.

The chapter on the Soviet Union was read by Harry Schwartz, of Syracuse University and the New York *Times,* and Professor David Granick, of Fisk University. Several other specialists in the problems of Eastern Europe were extremely helpful in the preparation of this chapter.

Dr. Hans Singer, of the New School of Social Research and the United Nations Secretariat, and Professor Marcus Fleming, of Columbia University, both at one time associated with the Labor Government, made helpful suggestions about the chapter on the United Kingdom.

In addition, Ernest Van den Haag, of the New School of Social Research, and Harold Wattel, of Hofstra College, commented on various parts of the manuscript. Mrs. Joan Ritz worked through the material with the special purpose of finding portions that might be difficult for laymen to understand; she also helped to clear up the difficult passages.

Everyone here mentioned helped to make this book far better than it otherwise would have been. For this, I thank them for myself, and on behalf of the reader and the publisher, who are almost as much in their debt as I.

West Hempstead, N. Y. Alfred R. Oxenfeldt
February, 1952

Contents

ECONOMIC SYSTEMS IN ACTION

The United States, the Soviet Union, and the United Kingdom

CHAPTER ONE

The Study of Alternative Economic Systems

The study of foreign economic systems is often regarded as either superfluous or dangerous—superfluous, because it is assumed that the United States has nothing to learn from other nations; dangerous, because some people might be persuaded that another type of economic system is better and be led into a disloyal allegiance. One is entitled to the first conclusion only after making a comparative study; the second confuses patriotism with unquestioning loyalty to particular economic arrangements.

The argument that the United States retain its existing economic system without considering alternatives is peculiarly out of step with most American views. As a people, we oppose standpattism. We pride ourselves on the number and rapidity of changes in our methods of production and in the kinds of goods we produce. We call these changes "improvements" and take them as signs of progress—and, indeed, most of them are. One might suppose that we would be too eager to try new economic arrangements.

I. EXISTING ECONOMIES RATHER THAN THEORETICAL SYSTEMS WILL BE STUDIED

We could for the purpose of our study analyze and compare economic systems that have been proposed by various writers. These proposed systems generally single out the major principles around which an economy might be organized, but they admittedly do not describe a "total" economy. We can speak of such proposals as "theoretical" systems or "pure" systems.

Everyone will admit that "pure" capitalism, "pure" socialism, and "pure" communism do not now exist anywhere. Most economists will agree that they never graced the earth and that they never will. There is considerable disagreement about how closely our economy resembles "pure" capitalism, how closely the Soviet economy resembles "pure" socialism or communism, and how closely the British economy resembles "pure" socialism. Important purposes can be served by analyses of theoretical economic systems, but the value of conclusions based upon such analyses to an understanding of existing systems is limited. If one wishes to compare "pure" capitalism with alternative economic systems, he is obliged to compare it with "pure" socialism and "pure" communism, and his conclusions would be scarcely applicable to actual economies.

It is no accident that real economies do not follow theoretical patterns. Theoretical economies generally do not take into full account such things as the necessity of making concessions to political expediency; the limitations of human intelligence, integrity, knowledge, and interest in economic and political circumstances; and the influence of unforeseen circumstances like wars, natural catastrophes, and accidents. Departure of an actual economy from the theoretical model is certain, and the degree of departure cannot be measured. *That one type of economy is better "theoretically" than another does not necessarily imply that functioning examples of that system are superior.*

When seeking measures to remedy particular defects in an economy, it is safer to study actual economies in their full complexity rather than theoretical systems. Often, untried measures are meritorious in theory and it is logical to try them, though some may fail in practice because of circumstances neglected in the theory. However, arrangements that have already been put to a test should hold no great shocks or surprises when tried elsewhere, even though they will not everywhere have exactly the same consequences.

II. PROBLEMS FACED IN STUDYING ALTERNATIVE SYSTEMS

A few cautions should be made explicit before examining the economies of the United States, the Soviet Union, and the United Kingdom. First, in the following discussion we shall speak in generalities. We cannot describe any economic system in full detail; if we did, we would confuse issues rather than illuminate them. Exceptions can be found to most of the generalizations that will be offered here, but those presented are believed to summarize accurately most specific cases. On many matters, however, we lack sufficient information to generalize with confidence. Readers should therefore note the basis upon which the generalizations rest and the degree of validity attributed to each by the author. Some represent little more than the author's personal impressions; these should be distinguished from and given far less weight than those based on a large body of reliable evidence.

Second, persons studying alternative economic systems must recognize the highly controversial nature of the subject. There are extremely few impartial and competent analyses of the subject, and the average layman has had access to none of them. Most of the sources available to the general public advocate a particular point of view.

Most readers will find statements here that differ from anything they have read before. They will be asked to consider points of view that have been rejected out of hand and even ridiculed in their usual media of information. This divergence of opinion, however, does not prove absolute objectivity on the part of the author. Everyone feels the pressures of the times. The writer has tried to make a careful and honest study and, if challenged, would sincerely and vehemently proclaim his complete impartiality. Nevertheless, let the reader beware. In considering a subject as controversial as the one here discussed, let him examine critically *whatever* he reads. We are dealing with matters unusually susceptible to emotional coloration. It is not logical to assume that this study is completely immune from environmental influences.

Third, the greatest difficulty faced in a study of alternative economic systems is to be found in the reader's own prejudice. Many people are afraid to make a dispassionate study of alternative economic systems, for if they depart far from prevailing opinion, they may endanger their sense of ease and belongingness with their neighbors, and sometimes even their very livelihood. It takes great effort to study foreign systems with impartiality; few persons will succeed fully in doing so. Nevertheless, the effort is worth while, for the greater the impartiality achieved, the closer will one approach full understanding.

III. BASES ON WHICH ECONOMIC SYSTEMS CAN BE COMPARED

What meaning can be attached to a comparison of capitalist, communist, and socialist economies? Are not economic systems so different in basic goals that comparisons are pointless?

All economic systems try to do the same thing. Their common goal is to furnish the things most desired by the population in ways that involve minimum sacrifice. All economic systems perform similar activities in pursuing this general goal. They produce, store, and distribute goods and services; they employ individuals and make use of natural resources. Considered as economic rather than ethical systems, capitalism, communism, and socialism can be compared according to how closely they approach their general goal and how efficiently they perform particular functions. The five major economic functions of any system are discussed below. Various economies can be compared according to the efficiency with which they perform each one. It is unlikely that any system will excel in all five, although that is not impossible.

1. Every economy should produce goods that will best satisfy the population. Man wants many things. In all "developed" countries, even prosperous persons have unfilled desires for material possessions. Barring an unforeseen change in personal attitudes—of the kind that might be brought about only by the general adoption of some new religion—we can anticipate only a continuation of the present situation in which appetites for material goods are almost insatiable.

Even the most richly endowed regions cannot provide everyone with everything he would like to have. As a result, it is necessary to pick and choose. When one cannot have everything, he must select among alternatives. To obtain clothing, one must forego other things that could have been acquired in its place. Hence, one major function of an economic system is to select the particular things to produce from among all things that might be produced. Accordingly, we will examine the economies of the United States, the Soviet Union, and the United Kingdom to see if the particular goods produced provide maximum satisfaction for the population.

2. Every economy should use the most efficient methods of production. An economy might produce the best possible combination of products in the best proportions, and still be poor because of methods

of production that yield an output smaller than could have been produced using equal amounts of labor, capital, and raw materials. Efficient use of resources, moreover, requires that involuntary idleness and "underemployment" of productive factors be minimized. Comparisons of economies must consider degree of unemployment and production methods.

3. Every economy should direct individuals into occupations where they are most productive. In addition to the production of the "right" products by the most efficient methods, a nation's standard of living depends upon whether people work at the jobs they can perform most efficiently. Output will be low if "square pegs" are put in "round holes," no matter what methods of production are used. Consequently, to evaluate an economy requires consideration of the manner in which individuals are directed into particular employments.

4. If output is distributed in a manner that affords a few people enormous luxury while everyone else knows only squalor, the economic system can hardly be adjudged efficient. An efficient economic system distributes income on some ethical basis, shares output in a manner that affords a high level of total satisfaction for the population as a whole, and encourages individuals to make the maximum productive contribution consistent with health and a happy social and psychological adjustment. Since all of these objectives of income distribution appear to be inconsistent with one another, the only thing for us to do is to try to strike a happy balance among them.

5. Every economy should create new methods of production and new products. An economy that efficiently exploits existing technological knowledge will still be left far behind unless it also develops new products that satisfy unfilled wants or finds increasingly efficient means of production. In short, an efficient economy is "progressive" and moves forward toward higher living standards through technological innovation. Accordingly, we shall examine the arrangements in the United States, the Soviet Union, and the United Kingdom to determine whether they are conducive to the development of new production techniques and new or improved products.

In judging an economic system, one must not only study efficiency but also evaluate the by-products in the political, social, and psychological spheres. *Economic arrangements must meet more than the test of economic efficiency.* An economic system that produces a large output of material goods but inevitably creates personal insecurity, suppresses natural impulses, restricts movement or expression, violates personal, moral, and ethical codes, or distributes most of the output to a few while the vast majority suffers cruel privation, such a system cannot be considered good—unless all alternative arrangements are worse.

The chapters that follow will examine three economic systems—those of the United States, the Soviet Union, and the United Kingdom—from the standpoint of efficiency and of their noneconomic consequences. Each economy will be examined separately. The three will not be compared directly, for to do so would obscure the essential unity of each system. Every economy is an organic whole in which the consequences of every arrangement depend largely upon the character of all other arrangements.

CHAPTER TWO

Capitalism in the United States

Most readers of the following pages will be far better informed about the American economy than about any other. Description will therefore be brief and the system's merits and accomplishments will be stated without elaboration. The main purpose of the discussion will be to set forth standards by which an economy's performance may be judged and to measure the American economy against these standards.

Since the American economy is the first to be discussed, it is impractical to compare it directly with the Soviet and British economies. Later chapters, however, will compare the three systems. In judging the American economic system in this chapter, then, we must use absolute standards, that is, we must compare it with the best performance imaginable. Even though other economic systems may be inferior to it, by using this standard we can discover ways in which its performance might be improved. *Superiority over other systems does not excuse remediable defects.* Nevertheless, it should be stressed that the American economy is charged here with defects that also exist in the Soviet Union and the United Kingdom to an even greater degree.

I. A GENERAL VIEW OF THE AMERICAN ECONOMY

The economic system of the United States was not fashioned after any particular model. It just "growed," undergoing change as individuals altered their methods of doing business and as local and federal legislatures enacted or abolished regulations. Despite the apparent lack of plan in the American economy there is an underlying rationale that leads many people to believe that it operates efficiently. The rationale, however, must not be mistaken for reality; at many points the resemblance is not at all close.

A] THE RATIONALE UNDERLYING THE AMERICAN ECONOMY

Insofar as the American economy is a system, it is a "price" and "profit" system. It allows individuals and businesses almost complete freedom to produce what they want, to employ any productive methods they desire, and to price their output and services as they wish. This condition is expected to result in an efficient economic system primarily because it incorporates a basic and simple principle ordinarily called "competition." In brief, the system is expected to achieve the results desired because of the strenuous efforts that most individuals make in order to gain something they desire. They will, it is argued, try to produce the goods that consumers desire most, for in that way they will obtain high prices for their output and be able to win customers away from rivals. They will produce as efficiently as they can, for the resultant savings will increase their personal incomes. They will enter occupations where they are relatively productive in order to command high incomes and will exert their greatest energies in production in order to gain promotion and increase their incomes. All individuals and businesses will strive to devise new methods of production and new products, for by so doing they increase the likelihood of beating out their rivals and of gaining fortune, and possibly fame, for themselves.

In addition, the freedom of each individual in a price and profit system is a curb on the abuse of freedom by others. Sellers who offer goods of poor quality are checked by sellers who offer goods of high quality. Sellers who overcharge will be frustrated by others who try to increase their share of the market by underselling their competitors. Workers who are not conscientious or who make excessive wage demands can do little damage, for they will, or so it is argued, lose their jobs to other workers who do superior work or accept lower wages, or to a machine which does the same work more cheaply.

Moreover, a price and profit system is relatively safe against the mistakes and miscalculations of any individual or small group. Economic decisions are highly decentralized. Millions of businessmen individually and independently decide what to produce; even larger numbers of workers decide what occupations to enter. If some of them make an error, or are derelict, the consequences will not be of major significance, because others will provide the kinds of goods needed.

Not only are errors likely to be less damaging in such an economy than in one where decisions are centralized; they are also less likely to occur. Individuals left to decide matters that determine their personal fortunes take their decisions seriously; moreover, they generally decide matters about which they are relatively well informed.

The price and profit system does more than build on the principle of competition, allow freedom to individuals, and decentralize decisions. It provides a delicately calibrated system of penalties and rewards. A price system allows individuals to express fine shades of preference for alternative products by indicating the penalties they will incur to obtain them. The penalty is the price they will pay, thereby revealing the strength of their desire for each product. Similarly, individuals seeking employment and owners of productive property or liquid funds can indicate their sacrifice in providing services by the compensation they demand. When heavy penalties attach to the consumption of particular products, consumers feel pressure to seek out alternatives that will give them greater satisfaction per dollar. Likewise, businessmen are under pressure to find the productive arrangements that keep their penalties (money costs) to a minimum. Ideally, a price system will fix penalties on the use of products and factors of production that provide just the desired pressure to cause economy in their use.

In sum, it is argued that a system based upon freedom to individuals in their productive activities will yield the following results: sellers will not charge much, if any, more than the minimum costs at which a product or service can be provided. Goods will be produced with maximum efficiency, with individuals taking employment where they are most productive and incur minimum personal sacrifice. Output will be distributed on the basis of productive contribution, and the dependence of monetary rewards upon productivity will induce everyone to exert himself to the utmost. Consumers will use their incomes in ways that give them the greatest satisfaction obtainable. Producers and consumers will use plentiful products rather than equally useful products that are scarce.

The foregoing explains why the American economic system—a price and profit system—might be expected to achieve excellent results in performing functions common to all economic systems. It represents the general rationale for the American economy; it is not offered as an accurate description, however. The major characteristics of the American economy are briefly listed below. These are general characteristics to which numerous exceptions can be found, and in the discussion that follows, the importance of the exceptions to the generalizations will become clear.

B] GENERAL CHARACTERISTICS OF THE AMERICAN ECONOMY

1. *There is private ownership of the means of production,* that is, individuals and not the government own most of the nation's factories, machinery, ships, railroads, natural-resource deposits, and the like.

2. *In their economic activities individuals strive primarily to obtain maximum money income.* People ordinarily use their productive equipment, their money savings, and their labor skills in ways that give them the highest money return.

3. *Most individuals are compelled to take outside employment in order to provide for even their minimum needs.* Only a small proportion of the population finds support by working with self-owned means of production. The majority can earn a livelihood only by taking employment with persons who own means of production.

4. *The basic economic "decisions" about what shall be produced, in what quantities, by what methods, and for whom are made through a "price system."* There is no central group of planners that decides what goods shall be produced and specifies techniques of production and the like. These decisions are decentralized.

5. *Production and sale of most goods and personal services occur under conditions of rivalry among* buyers and sellers, each of whom is pursuing his own self-interest.

6. *Individuals are compensated in accordance with their productivity,* their rewards depending primarily upon their ability to produce the kinds of things that other people desire, their own diligence, and the scarcity of the skills they possess.

7. *Compared with most other industrialized countries the United States government does not intervene to a large extent in business activity;* businessmen are relatively free to pursue any course of action they wish.

8. *Industrial plants and equipment are available in very large quantities in relation to the size of the labor force.* Production in the United States is very highly mechanized, partly because money capital is available to borrowers on relatively attractive terms.

No listing of general characteristics can give a full understanding of anything so complex as an economic system. The essence of an economic system is to be found in the interrelation of its many separate parts. Accordingly, a more complete and realistic—but still quite general—description of the American economy will be attempted along other lines. We shall try to explain how the basic economic problems are "solved" in the United States today.

II. HOW THE BASIC ECONOMIC PROBLEMS ARE SOLVED IN THE UNITED STATES

A] WHO DECIDES WHAT THINGS ARE TO BE PRODUCED?

In the United States, consumers are free to purchase whatever they choose within limits set by their incomes and the minor restrictions imposed by the government. The purchase of a very small number of products is either proscribed or limited by the government. The most important among them are sulfurous matches, harmful drugs and narcotics, and in some states intoxicating liquors. In addition, the government discourages consumption of some goods and services by putting taxes on them. (Although not all these taxes were imposed for the purpose of limiting consumption, they do have that effect.) For example, taxes on cigarettes, gasoline, liquor, luxuries, movies, and night clubs discourage the consumption of these goods and services. Conversely, the government encourages consumption of some goods and services by subsidizing them in whole or in part. Examples include some farm products, education, public housing, postage for periodicals and books, and aviation. On the whole, government limitation and encouragement of consumption is on a small scale. Businessmen are essentially free to offer whatever goods they wish, and consumers are at liberty to buy or reject them. *The original decision about what shall be produced is made by producers; their decisions, in turn, are based on what they expect to be able to sell to consumers.*

That consumers are free to purchase whatever they choose does not, however, mean that they make their selections on the basis of their own judgment. Moreover, free consumer choice cannot in itself be taken as proof that consumers buy the products that give them the greatest satisfaction obtainable from their expenditures. We shall explore the influences that dictate consumers' choices and in that way try to discover how well their choices reflect their own best interests.

1. *Are the "Right" Goods Produced?*

The overriding objective of all economic activity is the satisfaction of material wants. An economic system should therefore produce the goods and services that satisfy consumers better than any others that could have been made with the same effort and raw materials.

Note that this objective has been stated in terms of "satisfying the consumer." To speak of satisfying consumers is to imply that they have basic desires whose satisfaction contributes to good health or good spirits, and whose denial results in unhappiness, frustration, or impaired health. Moreover, to speak of satisfying the consumers implies that they should be free to purchase whatever they wish. It seems obvious that you can satisfy people best by giving them what they want.

It is on these grounds that most economists favor "consumer sovereignty," a condition wherein consumers dictate to producers what shall be produced. Since in the United States today consumers are at liberty to choose whatever they please, they appear to be sovereign. Unless they wish to do so, they need not buy anything. Producers who make things that few persons will buy feel the lash of the consumers' disfavor in the form of financial loss or even business failure.

The problem of deciding who determines what shall be produced is not settled by a discussion of consumer sovereignty. We must determine why certain products are selected for purchase. Consumers may simply do what others make them do.

2. *Why Do Consumers Purchase the Things They Do?*

Advertising is the most widely recognized factor in consumers' choices, since everyone knows that it is designed specifically to influence consumer behavior. Although it is impossible to measure exactly its effect in any specific case, all the evidence taken together shows that advertising often strongly influences consumers' choices, is moderately effective in most cases, and only rarely seems to have no influence upon consumers.

Many circumstances other than advertising influence consumer choices. By far the most important is the desire and pressure to "conform." Individuals tend to imitate the people around them both from conscious desire to be like others and because their notions of what is right and wrong, good and bad, beautiful and ugly depend upon what others do and think.

The obvious influence of advertising and the tendency of the individual to imitate and conform show clearly that the consumer does not decide "for himself" what he wants. Consumers' choices, to an extent as yet not specified, reflect outside influences. Their choices may not indicate basic needs or desires; indeed, consumers may choose things that do them harm. To what extent do consumers' purchases indicate their own best judgment, real need, and basic desire, and to what extent are they dictated by outside pressures?

Consumer selection of goods sometimes directly reflects basic needs as adjudged by consumers themselves. When persons are cold, they will purchase something to keep them warm. A person who has not eaten for several days will buy food rather than reducing pills—no matter how fashionable it is to be slim. However, if we wish to estimate accurately the comparative effect of "outside influences" and the recognition of their own basic needs upon consumers, we should have to find out what consumers would buy if they were entirely free from outside influences.

We realize that this is scarcely possible. No individuals have been, nor could they be, free from environmental influences, although these vary widely from place to place. We know, for example, of societies in which people have a far smaller appetite for goods than in our own.[1] Yet even in these societies, and certainly in the Soviet Union and the United Kingdom, outside pressures strongly influence consumers' choices. However, differences in economic systems can be expected to create differences in such influences.

Is it possible to determine how intelligent is the selection of goods to be produced in the United States? Specifically, is it possible to compare the things that are produced with the kinds of things that "should be" produced?

---

[1] The best current examples are to be found in underdeveloped countries, where it frequently is difficult to persuade people to work, once their most elementary material needs have been met. In developed countries, Hutterite and Mennonite communities are examples of consumer groups having very modest desires for material goods. See J. W. Eaton, R. J. Weil, and B. Kaplan, "The Hutterite Mental Health Study," *Mennonite Quarterly Review,* January, 1951, pp. 3–19.

3. *Do Consumers Buy the Best Products Available?*

It is impossible to know what consumers should buy, apart from goods that satisfy their most basic needs. For example, one might specify the number of calories and vitamins needed for health at minimum cost, but it does not follow from anything yet said that consumers "should" purchase food on the basis of cost alone. Therefore, we need some other standard by which to evaluate the validity or efficiency of consumers' choices that does not require a decision about what their basic preferences should be. *One possible standard is the degree to which they purchase the best available brand of a specific product.* That is, we will not question the validity of their decision to buy, say, shoes; we will only try to discover whether they purchase the particular brand of shoes that gives them *what they themselves* want from shoes at minimum cost. To the extent that consumers purchase goods inferior to others available at equal cost, we can conclude that they choose badly. Such a finding would suggest strongly that free consumer choice does not lead to the production of the *best variety of goods,* even as it does not result in the production of only the *best brands* of any product.[2]

The standard of evaluation stated above does not measure exactly the efficiency of free consumer choice in the United States today. However, it is the only one that can be applied on a factual basis at the present time.

A comparison of various brands of the same product according to their ability to satisfy the wants of discerning consumers reached the following conclusion: ". . . consumers of the products studied averaged about two thirds of the satisfaction per dollar of expenditure they might have obtained. Put another way, the results suggest that the average consumer of these products could have increased his satisfaction by 50 per cent if he had bought the best product rated by Consumers' Union." [3]

A comparison of the prices charged for brands of similar quality confirmed the foregoing results. It showed that the average consumer spent at least 56 per cent more than he needed to spend.[4] This study also showed that the relationship between price and quality was relatively weak. ". . . while more expensive brands are higher

[2] Distinguish carefully between products—like hats, autos, radios—and brands of a product—like Ford, Chevrolet, Plymouth.

[3] A. R. Oxenfeldt, "Consumer Knowledge: Its Measurement and Extent," *Review of Economics and Statistics,* November, 1950, p. 306.

[4] *Ibid.,* p. 309.

in quality than cheaper brands for most of the products studied, the reverse was frequently true. For 9 of the 35 products, the cheaper brands typically were of higher quality than more expensive ones." [5]

These results show clearly that consumers are not able to guard fully their own welfare, even judging by tests that they could be expected to meet fairly well. Consumer performance in selecting among alternative *brands* of particular products should be superior to their performance in choosing which products to purchase, since they could make brand comparisons themselves as well as study the results of research done by testing organizations. There is no method, however, for assessing the amount of satisfaction to be obtained from different patterns of expenditure among alternative products.

How great, then, is the error of the average consumer in his selection of products? Is he a wise or a stupid sovereign? The results reported show that he can scarcely be considered wise; the extent of his ignorance, however, can only be conjectured. It should be recognized that we cannot say at this point whether American consumers select goods more or less intelligently than consumers in the Soviet Union or the United Kingdom.

B] HOW ARE METHODS OF PRODUCTION SELECTED?

Businessmen are free to use almost any productive techniques they desire. Restrictions are placed on the methods they select primarily by the patent laws, which restrict the use of certain techniques and the production of certain items to those who hold a patent, and by the refusal of organized labor to permit productive devices which may endanger employee health or decrease employment.[6]

Some businessmen complain that they are "no longer the boss," and that they "must run the factory the way the union tells them to." For the most part, however, American unions prefer to leave the choice of productive methods to the employer.[7]

---

[5] *Ibid.*, p. 310.

[6] All factors of production affect productive techniques by requiring payment; the greater the payments they command, the greater the obstacle to their use. If all productive factors were free or received the same compensation, methods of production would be very different from what they are.

[7] In Europe, notably in Germany, a movement that has gained considerable headway admits labor representatives to great participation (approximately 50 per cent) in the top decision-making body of some large industrial corporations. This condition is termed "codetermination."

Generally speaking, production methods in the United States are selected by businessmen after an examination of alternatives. From among the alternative methods, businessmen select the one they believe will involve the lowest money cost over a moderately long period. The motive for selecting the least costly method of production is obvious; the lower the cost, the greater the profit, and also the smaller the likelihood that competitors will force one out of business altogether.

Does this method of selecting production methods result in an efficient economy? To answer this question, we must first decide what is meant by efficiency in production. Certainly it does not necessarily mean the use of the most modern and complicated types of machinery, for sometimes such methods require more workers, some of them more highly skilled than would be needed with less complex machinery.

Is efficiency to be judged by the number of labor hours used to produce a given output? Surely the answer must be negative, for a method that uses fewer man-hours than another, but which requires the most skilled workmen in the nation, would not be efficient. In addition to the number of man-hours worked, we must also take into account the labor skills used. But how can skills of different workmen be compared accurately?

How, then, shall we judge productive efficiency? Ideally, efficiency means that we "give up as little as possible." But *of what* must we give up as little as possible? We must give up as little as possible of other things that might be produced in place of the product in question.

There generally are many ways of producing the same thing. The most efficient method is the one that requires the smallest sacrifice of other things. An example might make this tricky notion clear. Consider *X* product that could be produced either by using 100 men of relatively low skill or by using 50 men of considerable skill. We can tell which method is more efficient only if we know what these men could have produced in other occupations. For the sake of simplicity, assume that the men could only be used in two occupations, in the *X* industry and to raise wheat. Assume further that the 100 men could raise 11,000 bushels of wheat per year, and that the 50 skilled men could raise 15,000 bushels. The method of producing *X* involving the 100 workers would entail the smaller cost. Their use would require us to give up less wheat than we would have lost by using the 50 skilled men. By using the 100 unskilled men to make *X*, we end up with 4,000 bushels more of wheat as well as the same amount of *X*.

In actual practice, workers' output of all alternate products cannot be measured. Consequently, no available yardstick permits accurate comparisons of the efficiency of different arrangements. One is driven to the use of yardsticks that are only rough approximations.

It has already been stated that businessmen base their decisions upon the yardstick of money costs. Unfortunately, this standard is frequently defective as a measure of what we must give up in order to produce something else. Inasmuch as this standard is widely used, some of its limitations will be listed.

The reasons for disparity between money costs and real costs are many. Certain groups of relatively unskilled workers are able to command high incomes because they use concerted action and even force to support their wage demands. While the output of these workers in alternative occupations is low, their money cost is high. In such a case, there is no close parallel between real cost and money cost. Similarly, some firms possess strong market power and the prices they charge for their products exaggerate the real costs of producing them. Also, some real costs involved in production are not borne by the producer of the end product, and accordingly are not included in his money costs. Examples of such real costs include: injury to health and inconvenience resulting from dirt, smells, noise, and traffic congestion that attend the production of some things. Persons in the neighborhood who suffer from these conditions are not compensated for their inconvenience or suffering. On the other hand, some producers incur money costs that are disproportionately high in relation to real costs. The most common excessive costs found in industry include: exorbitant managerial compensation where a firm is under control of nonowning managers; the preferential hiring of friends or relatives, even though more efficient employees are available at the same salary; failure to seek out or adopt improved production techniques; purchase of products from friends or relatives at higher prices or of lower quality than merchandise available elsewhere.

Further disparity between money and real costs results from inadequate opportunities for education and training for the poor, with a resultant overcrowding of the market for unskilled labor. The low pay commanded by unskilled labor therefore tends to understate substantially the real cost of that labor to society.

Even though money costs have grievous defects as measures of real costs, they generally are the best measure available. Frequently, we must use them for want of something better, knowing that we may err. As far as possible, we must concentrate on real rather than money costs in evaluating productive efficiency.

If we take money costs to be an accurate measure of productive efficiency, to what extent are businessmen efficient? Do they keep their costs at a minimum? Do they know the cost of alternative production methods? How hard do they try to keep money costs to a minimum?

Businessmen insist that they make strong efforts to seek out the least costly methods of production. It seems, however, that some men who determine what methods of production should be employed have only a weak incentive to minimize costs. There is evidence that those who manage large corporations do not personally bear the losses from bad or unlucky decisions, and they also do not share heavily in profits resulting from good or lucky decisions. Should those executives who do not personally feel the impact of their decisions be expected to pursue corporation profits aggressively? Frequently the answer is *no.* To be as efficient as possible involves management in added effort and often in added risk of financial loss. Considerable evidence suggests that the zeal with which businessmen devote themselves to the pursuit of productive efficiency varies. When their firms have experienced financial losses, managements have generally found ways of reducing their costs significantly.[8]

It thus appears that productive methods often are less efficient than businessmen could make them. Inefficiency arises partly from lack of strong pressure to attain maximum efficiency; no doubt it results in part also from the impossibility of learning what the most efficient methods are.

Up to this point we have assumed that the businessman himself determines what productive methods to use, subject only to minor limitations by government and labor unions. Actually, a businessman's methods are strongly conditioned by the activities of his competitors. A businessman who knows the most efficient method

[8] For examples, see A. R. Oxenfeldt, *Industrial Pricing and Market Practices* (New York: Prentice-Hall, Inc., 1951), pp. 117, 120–121.

of conducting his business may be unable to employ that method because of circumstances beyond his control. For example, consider a retailer who sets up his shop most efficiently, but finds that due to the advent of many new competitors his store never operates at full efficiency. The additional stores might cause his productive facilities to be excessive. Or, on the other hand, the competition might lower prices and force a businessman to produce more efficiently in order to survive. Businessmen are also limited in the productive methods they use by the size of their capital resources. Sometimes they must forego the use of more efficient methods because they cannot pay for the new facilities required. Labor unions also influence productive methods, sometimes obstructing the use of new techniques, sometimes pressing for greater efficiency.

In assessing current productive efficiency in the United States, it is helpful to examine separately raw-material extraction, agriculture, manufacturing, and distribution. We will find uneven levels of productive efficiency in these various fields.

1. *Degree of Productive Efficiency in Raw-Material Industries*

Efficient raw-material industries must meet four major conditions: First, raw materials must be extracted from the ground by use of minimum productive resources. Second, the rate at which raw materials are used up must be such that later generations are not deprived of valuable resources for the sake of a trivial gain to the present generation. Third, the resources provided by nature must be "used to the full," and no economically removable portion of the resource should be left in the ground unless it can be recaptured later. Fourth, materials should be reused as far as economically feasible.

Each of these criteria must be applied in an economic rather than a physical sense. It would be foolhardy to use methods of extraction that leave absolutely no raw materials in the ground. Even if such methods existed, they would almost invariably be enormously costly. To use all reusable raw materials would also involve very heavy costs; one would choose to reclaim only those materials that were readily accessible and of high value. The best possible use of a resource over a period of time poses special problems. It requires an estimate of future needs as well as of available future supplies.

Since the criteria of productive efficiency in raw-material industries are difficult to apply, we must content ourselves with a very superficial discussion of this problem. As in other cases where information is not available or where the subject is highly controversial, conflicting arguments of recognized validity will be summarized.

A] Claims for the Raw-Material Industries.

1. The raw-material industries have been extremely diligent in prospecting for new raw-material deposits.

2. Raw-material industries in the United States are more highly mechanized than in any other nation.

3. Raw-material industries have made improvements in technology by virtue of extensive research efforts.

B] Charges against the Raw-Material Industries.

1. Raw materials are extracted with reference to profitability alone. As a result, there is little regard for wastes in extraction. Raw materials are extracted in ways that aim to minimize money costs and in so doing a substantial quantity of raw materials has been either unnecessarily destroyed or rendered unrecoverable. The petroleum, coal, and lumber industries have been the chief offenders.[9]

2. The industries producing raw materials have erred on the side of using up our natural resources at too rapid a rate.

3. Prospecting for new deposits of raw materials has been highly inefficient. Too many persons, many using primitive methods, are engaged in the search for raw materials, when it could be organized and made systematic and more efficient.[10]

2. *Productive Efficiency in Agriculture*

Agriculture is the largest single economic activity in the United States. In 1948, approximately 8 million persons, out of about 59 million who were employed in all lines of activity,[11] were engaged in agriculture. Agricultural employment thus accounted for over 13 per cent of total employment. This fundamental line of economic activity is characterized by low productive efficiency.

Amercan agriculture ties up far more people on farms than are

---

[9] For a discussion of the manner in which resources were wasted, see "A National Plan for American Forestry," *Senate Document* No. 12, 73 Cong., 1 Sess., 1933. See also G. T. Renner and W. H. Hartley, *Conservation and Citizenship* (Boston: D. C. Heath & Company, 1940), pp. 80–89, 230–232.

[10] For an illuminating and factual discussion of prospecting and extraction in the oil industry, see "Hearings of the Temporary National Economic Committee," Part 14, pp. 7379–7404.

[11] *Statistical Abstract of the United States,* 1949, p. 176.

needed to produce the desired output. A very extensive survey of agricultural methods reached the following conclusion: "If the workers in . . . rural families could be employed at jobs where they would produce as much as the average worker on the medium-sized commercial family farm or the average rural nonfarm worker, the production and output of rural people would be increased 20 to 25 per cent. This is the equivalent of adding 2,500,000 workers to the total labor force."[12] Note that the standard of comparison used is not farms of highest productivity, but only the average. Accordingly, the estimates of losses in output or manpower due to use of inefficient production methods and to the unnecessarily large amount of labor tied up in agriculture are extremely conservative. It is inevitable that farmers sometimes will have little work to do and at other times will be extraordinarily busy. The estimate of a possible increase of 20 to 25 per cent accepts as necessary and inevitable the average loss of working time now sustained on the average medium-sized commercial family farm. Of course some differences in productivity must be anticipated in agriculture due to variations in soil fertility and the beneficence of the elements.

Another indictment of American agriculture is that it wantonly wastes soil fertility. Reliable studies have disclosed that agricultural methods in the United States have permitted the loss of precious topsoil and the exhaustion of soil minerals needed to raise crops.[13] Huge areas of the United States were farmed without regard to the social value of arable land. Cotton and tobacco farmers were compelled to move westward from the Eastern seaboard as they depleted the soil fertility by exploitative agricultural methods. Dust storms, more serious previously than now but still not confined to the past, result from farming methods and deforestation that literally allow a vital natural resource to blow away.

While many farms are highly mechanized and most agriculture now is conducted by methods that restore soil fertility, agriculture in the United States is still relatively inefficient. Important strides have been made, primarily under government auspices, to teach the best farming methods and to encourage farmers to give up

---

[12] Joint Committee on the Economic Report, *Underemployment of Rural Families*, 82 Cong., 1 Sess., 1951, pp. 4, 5.

[13] See Fairfield Osborn, *Our Plundered Planet* (Boston: Little, Brown & Company, 1948), and Renner and Hartley, *op. cit.*, pp. 107–137.

low-quality farmland. Much progress remains to be made before American agriculture approaches the productivity of manufacturing industries.

3. *Efficiency in Manufacturing Industries*

In assessing the efficiency of manufacturing, we want to know about the amount of facilities available and the degree of skill and efficiency with which they are put to use. Studies of manufacturing capacity show two conflicting situations. Some industries seem able to produce far more goods than could be sold *even if the economy were fully employed,* that is, far more than they could reasonably hope to sell. Such industries attract new producers for a variety of reasons and end up with excessive facilities. Measurement of excess capacity is crude at best,[14] but there is undivided agreement that some industries have excessive manufacturing facilities.[15]

Other industries have fewer productive facilities than seem necessary to meet the nation's peak demands. Businessmen in those industries, either independently, by agreement, or out of mutual awareness of their common interests, refrain from expanding facilities. Industries that limit productive facilities cannot be charged with the wastes of excessive capacity. They may be guilty of the perhaps graver waste of underproduction.

With what skill and efficiency are American manufacturing facilities put to use? Two types of evidence bear on this question. First, we could compare American methods with those of other nations. By this standard, American manufacturing industries are unquestionably the most efficient in the world. America's manufacturing processes have received more praise, sometimes in the form of imitation, than any other branch of American industry.

Second, we can compare our productive methods with the most efficient that might be used. This second test is complex and will take a little explaining. Consider the case of a businessman who

---

[14] Some of the difficulties in measuring excess capacity can be listed: some idle capacity is warranted by uncertainty of the size of markets and danger that facilities might break down. More important, it is impossible to build new facilities at the same rate that consumption expands, for generally facilities must be added in big lumps—that is, a whole new plant must be built or a new deposit must be mined. Accordingly, there would ordinarily be, even under the best circumstances, some idle facilities until demand caught up with the expansion.

[15] An outstanding example is the whisky distilling industry with productive capacity more than five times the annual output of whisky. See Oxenfeldt, *Industrial Pricing and Market Practices,* p. 451.

has been producing inefficiently, but who is not aware of his competitors' superior methods. Assume that he is at liberty to use the superior methods. If this man had been diligent—if he had kept abreast of technical developments or had hired engineering consultants—he would have learned of these methods. We would consider this man inefficient.

The wide variation in the apparent efficiency of individual firms in the same industry suggests that some firms use relatively inefficient techniques. Differences in efficiency, however, are not proof of inefficiency. It would be wasteful from the individual businessman's point of view and for society as a whole to discard existing equipment every time an improvement in productive methods is made. When improvements are made, the economies they make possible must be set against the losses of scrapping equipment. The losses may exceed the gains, in which event the firm should continue to use the old techniques. However, despite the difficulty of interpreting differences in techniques in the same industry, businessmen and labor union officials agree that the efficency of firms in an industry, however measured, often varies widely. In addition, a study of waste in American industry in 1921 by a committee of engineers[16] turned up evidence of considerable and widespread inefficiency. While no similar survey has been made recently, there is no reason to believe the situation has changed radically.

Another reason for suspecting that productive methods are not as efficient as they might be has already been suggested. American firms characteristically make substantial improvements in productive methods under pressure—as during depression and price wars. Presumably, efficient managements would have made these improvements in the absence of strong pressure.

4. *Productive Efficiency in Retailing*

Few kind words have been said about the efficiency of distribution in the United States. The high proportion of each retail sales dollar that goes for distribution has excited considerable agitation in this country. Some industries—especially gasoline retailing—have become public jokes. Gas stations on several corners of an intersection are commonplace. Many other lines of retailing—such as liquor,

[16] *Waste in Industry,* Committee on Elimination of Waste in Industry, Federated American Engineering Societies (Washington, 1921). See also Stuart Chase, *The Tragedy of Waste* (New York: The Macmillan Company, 1927), especially pp. 145–174.

shoe, hat, and drug stores—seem to have visibly excessive facilities in most communities. Duplication of retail facilities apparently is the general rule.[17]

In assessing the efficiency of retailing, difficulties are faced in obtaining desired information and in devising reliable criteria. Can we be certain that there are too many gas stations? If so, what standards are we applying? Even if we grant that gas station facilities are excessive, how large is the excess? No demonstrably correct answers to these questions are possible. There is little we can do here but again rely on observation and "common sense." Both are treacherous, but we have no choice. Common observation, common sense, and the views of specialists indicate that retailing is relatively inefficient in the United States, at least in regard to excessive facilities.

5. *Productive Efficiency and the Full Utilization of Resources*

In assessing the productive efficiency of an economic system, its ability to use all resources available is of paramount importance. To use *employed resources* efficiently but to leave a substantial proportion of all resources unemployed is to save with one hand what is wasted with the other.

American capitalism has wasted considerable resources through unemployment. Between 1930 and 1939, an extreme but fairly recent example, about $390 billion of output measured in 1946 prices was wasted through unemployment.[18] The short recession—sometimes called a period of readjustment—in the early part of 1949 resulted in almost 5 million unemployed persons. Few people dispute the fact that the level of total activity in American capitalism is quite unstable. Although fluctuations in employment since 1941 have not been great, due to disturbed international relations including war, there is no reason to believe that the threat of unemployment has been ended forever. On the contrary, no basic changes in our economy have occurred since 1937—the year of the last major downswing—that would justify the view that Amercan capitalism will never again suffer from major depressions.

---

[17] In 1935, for example, about 60 per cent of all retail stores had a daily sales volume of less than $33. See The Twentieth Century Fund, *Does Distribution Cost Too Much?* (New York: 1939), pp. 49 and 299.

[18] Theodore Morgan, *Introduction to Economics* (New York: Prentice-Hall, Inc., 1950), p. 510.

Failure to eliminate unemployment is attributable to the inability to maintain a level of expenditure that, at existing price levels, would buy the output of all people desiring to work. (A related idea is generally expressed as the failure to prevent an excess of savings over investment. If savings and investment were equal, the total level of expenditure would remain what it was in the preceding period and no *new* unemployment would occur, assuming the average level of prices to remain unchanged.) Actually, full employment is not assured by the maintenance of equality between savings and investment, or the continuation of past levels of expenditure. Some mechanism is also needed that will absorb increments to the labor force.

Failure even to maintain equality of savings and investment is at least partly due to the absence of any centralized agency whose function is to create such an equality. Savings are made by millions of individuals and businesses operating independently; investment is also the result of the decisions of millions of independent individuals, businesses, and government units. An equality between their savings and investments would be an extraordinary accident.

Measures are at hand that would combat downswings in output and employment. Moreover, they are quite compatible with the fundamental principles underlying a price and profit system of the American type. Until these measures are adopted, however, the American economy must be charged with the major defect of cyclical unemployment, which entails enormous economic and perhaps even greater noneconomic costs.

C] THE ALLOCATION OF PRODUCTIVE AGENTS AMONG OCCUPATIONS

1. *Who Decides Where Productive Agents Shall Be Employed?*

In the United States, each worker and each owner of property and funds is at liberty to use his services and property as he wishes. The government places only slight obstacles in his way. These obstacles may take the form of zoning restrictions, which limit the uses to which land and property may be put; or the government may outlaw certain occupations such as gambling, the production of liquor and dangerous products, and prostitution. Restrictions on free occupational choice have been erected by some organizations of laborers and professional workers. Ordinarily these restrictions set unnecessarily high requirements for entrance into a union or for certification as a member of a profession. Moreover, some positions, often the most remunerative and socially important, are pre-empted by persons with personal and political influence. In addition to these limits on occupational choice, some positions are closed to workers on grounds of race or religion. Possibly the greatest limitation on free occupational choice results from a lack of jobs during depression. How do workers and owners of other productive agents decide what employment to accept—when they have a choice?

The following discussion is phrased in terms of only one factor of production—labor—because labor, measured by any index, is by far the most important productive factor. What is said about labor is substantially but not exactly valid for the other factors. Put differently, land, liquid funds, and natural resources probably are divided among alternative employments more efficiently than is labor.

2. *What Employments Will Workers Favor?*

One would expect labor to select the employment giving it the greatest "net advantages," that is, employment in which the combined money income and nonmonetary aspects of the job give the greatest return. A hypothetical illustration will make clear what is meant by "net advantages."

Consider a worker who could earn $100, $90, and $85 in the three highest paying positions he can obtain. We will assume, realistically, that he does not like all three jobs equally. Assume also for illustrative purposes that the worker likes the highest paying employment least and prefers the employment paying $90 a week to the point of being willing to give up $20 a week to work there rather than work in the highest paying job. He may prefer the second job because he finds the activities more pleasant, because he likes his associates on that job more, or because the position is more secure or offers greater opportunity for advancement; the particular source of his preference need not concern us. These conditions are described in Table 2-1.

The greatest net advantage to the worker is to be obtained in occupation No. 2. There he would obtain the equivalent of $110 in comparison with the $100 obtainable in occupation No. 1—and $95 obtainable in occupation No. 3. If the worker knew about the three positions and could accurately predict his reactions to work-

TABLE 2-1

A Comparison of Net Advantages in Three Hypothetical Occupations

Occupation	Weekly pay	Amount of weekly income worker would be willing to give up to work in corresponding occupation rather than in occupation No. 1	Net advantages
No. 1	$100	....	$100
No. 2	90	$20	110
No. 3	85	10	95

ing in them, he would select occupation No. 2, for it would make him better off than either of the other two.

While we would expect each factor of production to prefer the occupation offering the greatest net advantages, we must inquire into how productive factors actually do select the occupations they enter. We want to know whether or not workers get into suitable employments. It should be manifest that the proper allocation of productive factors among occupations is vital to the productive efficiency of any economic system.

3. *Where Should Workers Be Employed?*

By what standards can the suitability of an occupation for a particular productive factor be judged? We can identify the personal point of view—which, as indicated, would afford each individual maximum net advantages. The second point of view to be distinguished is that of the nation as a whole and is termed the "social viewpoint." What difference, if any, exists between the personal and social viewpoints concerning where a factor of production should be employed?

From the social viewpoint, there are two determinants of the suitability of an occupation for a factor of production. First, a worker should be employed where his output is greatest. (By output, we mean value of output rather than physical output; it is impossible to compare products in terms of units; how shall we compare the production of thirty neckties with the growing of two bushels of wheat?) Second, productive factors should, as far as possible, enter occupations where their net personal sacrifice is at a minimum. Personal sacrifice might take the form of doing work that is injurious to health, violates moral principles, or is distasteful on any other grounds.

If the output of a worker were high in an occupation that he found distasteful, what should be done? In general, added pleasurability must be balanced against lower income. A specific illustration could be fashioned out of the information presented in Table 2-1. If the net contribution to output were measured by the amount an employer pays a worker,[19] then the worker should, from the social viewpoint, still enter employment No. 2. Society has no right, nor should it have the desire, to require individuals to work in employments without regard to their tastes. Therefore, there need be no conflict between the choice of occupations by individuals on the basis of net advantages and what is best from the social viewpoint.

4. *Do Workers Enter the Occupations They Should?*

It is well recognized that workers prefer high-paying jobs to those that pay poorly. Consequently, many workers try to enter employments that pay high incomes. Those occupations, therefore, have the pick of the best workers. We must inquire whether it is desirable that the best workers go into occupations that pay best. Does the pay of a job indicate the importance of that job to society?

A] Is the Pay of an Employment an Indicator of Its Social Importance? Rates of pay in any occupation are determined by a variety of factors. They primarily depend upon the scarcity of the skill that is required—that is, the intensity of competition among productive factors for the available jobs, the costs of training, the relative market power of workers and employers, and the amount that buyers are willing to pay for the thing that is produced. Of these factors, the relative market power of employer and worker often is the most important, although there is no necessary connection between market power and the importance of a job to society. The other determinants of wage rates—particularly the amount that buyers are willing to pay for the product—clearly reflect the value of the job to society.

Scarce factors of production generally fetch a high price. For example, the high pay of prize fighters can be taken as evidence of social contribution. It can be argued that a successful prize fighter's pay is high because a large number of people are so interested in

[19] The validity of this assumption is open to serious question.

fighting that they will pay substantial sums to see him perform. Whether one likes to watch fights or not, he is forced to concede that the skilled professional fighter serves the large number of people who do. In almost all cases, the payment of large incomes to productive factors is accompanied by large consumer payments for the things that those factors produce.

If the money income obtainable from a job does not always measure its value to society, what other criterion could be used? No alternative has been advanced, which is not surprising in view of the large number and complexity of factors that enter into measuring the social importance of a job. However, absence of a better measure is no justification for taking the one available to us as fully accurate. We should recognize that rates of pay in individual occupations are determined to a large extent by factors that are irrelevant to social contribution—particularly market power. Since people pick jobs primarily on the basis of rates of pay (from among available jobs for which they have the requisite skills), they may enter occupations where their contributions to total output will be lower than they would be in some other occupation.

B] Do Productive Factors Know Alternative Employments They Might Obtain? If workers are to take the jobs among those open to them that offer the highest net advantages, they must know their job opportunities.[20] Do workers have the time necessary to canvass carefully the job opportunities in their own communities? Do they make an effort to learn and follow up opportunities in distant communities? For many persons, the answer seems to be a decided negative. People seem to learn about jobs mostly in accidental ways; systematic job seeking seems to be the exception rather than the rule.

The development of employment agencies—especially under government auspices—has greatly improved the situation. However, many employers do not make use of public employment services in hiring and, partly for that reason, many workers do not do so either. To explore carefully all job opportunities in even a small community takes considerable time and effort. If this time and effort were applied to a job about which one has already heard, it would

[20] Of course, workers cannot be expected to know *all* jobs they might obtain. Due to the high costs in time and effort of obtaining detailed knowledge of employment opportunities, it is not even socially desirable that workers know *all* job alternatives open to them.

yield income. Workers who are under pressure to obtain steady income probably do not canvass the job market carefully. While they may use an employment service to obtain jobs, workers rarely take the time to canvass employments that the placement services do not tell them about.

c] Do Workers Have the Opportunity to Develop Their Productive Capacities? If workers are to enter the employments for which they are best suited, individuals must have a chance to develop their abilities for the jobs where their talents can serve the community best. Do individuals in the United States have the opportunity to develop their greatest productive skill?

A reliable answer to this question cannot be expected, because it is impossible to measure latent talents. Some studies that are indicative of the degree of opportunity for developing productive talents are those reporting on the opportunities of superior high-school students to obtain college training. A college education is not needed to develop all kinds of talent. However, those students with outstanding academic records in high school are likely to be best suited for occupations for which a college education is necessary.

One study of over 4,000 high-school students who were classified by intelligence and size of parents' income obtained striking results. It showed that "all economic groups except the highest salaried group are represented in the highest one percentile class" (that is, students in the top 1 per cent ranked according to intelligence). "Many of the most superior group of high-school seniors will not attend college, while those with the most inferior grades of intelligence are planning to attend, in ever increasing numbers. Twenty-five per cent of the brightest seniors found in the entire State said they were not planning to attend college at all, while 65 to 70 per cent of the dullest seniors had definitely decided to go to college, most of them [having] already selected the college they expected to attend." [21]

Other similar studies show that brains are not closely correlated with personal income. Opportunities for development of native ability depend heavily upon one's financial resources. While scholarships help some exceptionally talented persons of low income, they

---

[21] Quoted from Vannevar Bush, *Science the Endless Frontier* (Washington: Government Printing Office, 1945), pp. 167–168. In turn, it is taken from William F. Book, *The Intelligence of High School Seniors* (New York: The Macmillan Company, 1928), pp. 216 and 298.

are given to an extremely small proportion of all needy and able students.[22] Furthermore, the most needy students require more than scholarship aid; they must supplement the family income as soon as possible.

It thus appears that in America many extremely able persons do not have the opportunity to attain the highest positions for which their native talents fit them. Inability to obtain the required training compels many of these persons to take unskilled positions. Society thus loses the benefit of their rare potential skills.

However, academic training is not a requisite for success in all employments. It is needed primarily for the professions. Access to training needed to become a skilled manual worker almost certainly is more generally and equally available than professional training.

In addition to unequal opportunity to develop skills, there are important inequalities in job opportunities for equally skilled persons. Nepotism is commonplace. Indeed, many fathers are spurred on in their business efforts to "make a business for the children to take over." Those who "choose the right father" typically occupy better jobs and have higher incomes than many more talented persons.

Furthermore, as already noted, many lines of work are closed to persons on the basis of considerations irrelevant to their economic performance. Members of minority groups are relegated to occupations requiring less skill than those for which they may be best suited. Members of the majority group get first pick and often occupy posts for which they are less suited than some members of minority groups. As a result, society is denied output that would be produced if the best person filled each job.

No reliable quantitative estimate can be made of the output lost due to unequal opportunity in the United States. In some respects, opportunity to get ahead is becoming more equal. The GI Bill of Rights probably has given a big boost to talented persons who otherwise would have been compelled to take unskilled jobs. Prejudice against minority groups seems on the decline, though it is far from absent.[23] Partly offsetting these developments is the tendency to increase the time and the cost required to become highly

[22] Scholarships and fellowships in 1951 provided free tuition for about one student in twenty. See results of a survey by the U.S. Office of Education reported in *Time Magazine,* December 24, 1951, p. 40.

[23] Between the end of World War II and 1951, religious and racial prejudice declined an estimated 40 per cent. This result is based upon an extensive survey reported in *New York Times,* October 20, 1951, p. 17.

skilled in a trade or profession. On balance, it seems that the output lost because of unequal opportunity for individuals to develop and to use their productive talents is still substantial.

D] THE DISTRIBUTION OF PERSONAL INCOME IN THE UNITED STATES

The distribution of personal income in the United States is quite unequal. Several factors determine the income that any individual receives. They are: (1) productivity—that is, the ability to produce goods that buyers want; (2) personal property holdings—that is, income in the form of profits, interest, and dividends; (3) market power—the ability to raise the price one obtains by exerting economic or physical force; (4) social services obtained from the government, such as social insurance, pensions, bonuses, etc.; (5) personal and political influence—including "pull" and "contacts" that permit a person to obtain a desirable job even though there are superior candidates for it; and (6) the opportunity one has to develop his productive capabilities to the full.

The most important question to raise regarding the distribution of income is, Do we distribute income in a manner that affords maximum net satisfaction to the population as a whole? That is, after taking into account the effects of income distribution on incentive—and therefore upon total output—is income so distributed that the nation as a whole is better satisfied than it could be with any other distribution of income? As with the other questions we have raised, no reliable answer can be given to this one. Further income redistribution without lowering incentive seems possible on the basis of the British experience, to be discussed presently, and the response of the American economy to substantial increases in tax rates since 1933. Greater equality—though not full equality—conceivably might increase rather than lower total output. We simply do not know enough about human reactions to estimate the effect of moderate changes in potential net money income upon most productive efforts.

The government does not allow everyone to keep all the income he receives. A major influence upon the amount of income one may dispose of as he wishes is the character of income tax legislation. Table 2-2 indicates the effect of federal income taxes upon the distribution of personal income in 1949. It should be noted that the very poorest spending units, with incomes below $1,000, did not improve their relative position because of income taxes. All others did, at the expense of spending units with incomes over $5,000.

TABLE 2-2

Effect of Federal Income Tax on Distribution of Income, 1949

Income group	Spending units		Total money income	
	Before tax	After tax	Before tax	After tax
Under $1,000	14	15	2	2
$1,000–$1,999	19	21	9	11
2,000– 2,999	21	22	16	19
3,000– 3,999	19	18	19	21
4,000– 4,999	11	11	15	16
5,000– 7,499	11	8	19	16
7,500 and over	5	5	20	15
All groups	100	100	100	100

SOURCE: *Federal Reserve Bulletin*, August, 1950, p. 960.

Clearly income inequality in the United States is substantial, though it is not, as it was in 1929, greater than in any other nation for which a comparable calculation could be made; [24] since then the United States has considerably reduced income inequality after taxes (Table 2-3). As Table 2-3 indicates, the richest fifth of the American population suffered a cut in its share of total personal income by over one seventh between 1935–1936 and 1949. The share of total personal income received by poor persons and persons of modest means increased correspondingly. Concurrent with this shift in the distribution of personal incomes, there was a substantial rise in total income. Accordingly, the low income groups improved their absolute situation even more than the table suggests. Similarly, the richest fifth of all spending units probably was better off in absolute terms in 1949, as compared with their situation in 1935–1936.

Unquestionably great strides toward income equality have

[24] Colin Clark, *The Conditions of Economic Progress* (London: Macmillan & Co., Ltd., 1940), p. 425.

TABLE 2-3

Distribution of Personal Income before Income Taxes in the United States, 1941, 1948, 1949*

Spending units arranged by size of income	Percentage of net income accounted for by each fifth of the population			
	1935–1936	1941	1948	1949
Lowest fifth	4	3	4	4
Second fifth	9	9	11	11
Third fifth	14	16	16	17
Fourth fifth	20	22	22	23
Highest fifth	53	50	47	45
All groups	100	100	100	100

* These data report incomes of "spending units," including as separate units both families and individuals who do not pool their incomes with their families, even though living with them, and single persons living alone.

SOURCE: Council of Economic Advisers, *Annual Economic Review,* January, 1950, p. 144, and January, 1951, p. 229.

been made since the early 1930's. Nevertheless, personal poverty has not been eliminated by any means. Due to the greatly increased income equality, the cure for poverty must now be sought more in methods of increasing output than in further redistributions of existing output. Even during years of unparalleled prosperity such as 1947 and 1948, the total income produced in the United States would not provide what most Americans regard as a "decent" standard of living, *even if income were equally divided.* To combat poverty, therefore, effort must be concentrated primarily on measures for keeping the economy progressive, eliminating restrictions on output, equalizing opportunities for training, and correcting production inefficiencies. Perhaps, too, it is imperative to guard against relapse into the great inequality of only a few decades back. The recent redistribution of income cannot be taken completely for granted.

E] PROGRESSIVENESS OF THE AMERICAN ECONOMY

Economic systems should provide the highest living standards possible under existing circumstances. In addition, they should improve prevailing circumstances. That is, the major functions of an economic system include the improvement of production techniques and the creation of products to satisfy desires in new ways.

Although over short periods the progressiveness of an economy will not add a great deal to economic welfare, over long periods it is a major determinant of living standards. An economy that can average a 2 per cent rise in productivity (output per man-hour) will double total output in about thirty years. An economy that fails to make such improvements will in a relatively short time fall far behind those that do. It may therefore be a mistake for a country to jeopardize its chances to improve production techniques and to create new products in order to, say, make income distribution somewhat more equitable. In time, if the economy were made less progressive, the condition of *even the poorest* members of the community would have been worsened as compared with what it would have been if the economy were progressive and income distribution were less equal.

Progress, as we have defined it, calls primarily for the creation of ideas for improved production techniques and for new products. The conscious production of new ideas is termed "research," and it is generally agreed that most worth-while new ideas are not discovered by complete accident or by sheer inspiration.[25] At the base of almost all important recent developments is painstaking and expensive research. How is the volume of research effort determined in the United States? How do our expenditures for research compare with those of other countries?

Before we try to answer these questions, one common source of misunderstanding should be cleared up. Nations with the most modern productive methods are not necessarily the most progressive. Progressive methods may be attributable to the possession of large financial resources rather than to the generation of new ideas. Prosperous nations often can carry out the development made in other nations better than those nations themselves. Our interest will be directed solely to research activity and the discovery of new ideas;

---

[25] Dr. Alfred N. Whitehead considered the discovery of the "art of invention" the greatest invention of the nineteenth century. He was referring to the fact that modern inventions most commonly arise from a routine and systematic application of elaborate chemical and mathematical formulae. See A. N. Whitehead, *Science and the Modern World* (New York: The Macmillan Company, 1925).

our earlier discussion of productive efficiency has already covered the efficiency of American productive techniques.

Total expenditures for technical research and development between 1930 and 1940 are presented in the following table. The peak reached before World War II was $345 million, which amounted to less than one half of 1 per cent of the total national income. The table indicates that the major source of expenditures for research and development before 1941 was private industry, which accounted for approximately two thirds of the total.

TABLE 2-4

National Research and Development Expenditures, 1930–1940
(Total amount and percentage of total)

Year	Federal government	Industry	Universities	Other	Total expenditures (in millions)
1930	14%	70%	12%	4%	$166
1932	20	63	13	4	191
1934	12	73	11	4	172
1936	15	70	11	4	218
1938	18	67	11	4	264
1940	19	68	9	4	345

SOURCE: "Science and Public Policy," report by the President's Scientific Research Board, August, 1947, vol. I, p. 10.

Expenditures for research following World War II took a sudden turn upward, and their sources also changed. The following table describes their amount, classified by source and according to whether they went for basic research or for applied research and development. It shows that the federal government is the chief source of all types of research expenditure at present.

After a very extensive survey of research activities in the United States, a distinguished group of scientists and government administrators under the chairmanship of John R. Steelman reached the following conclusions:

1. "In the past, our country has made less than its proportionate contribution to the progress of basic science. Instead, we have imported our theory from abroad and concentrated on its application

TABLE 2-5

The National Research and Development Budget (Excluding Atomic Energy), 1947
(In millions of dollars)

Agency	Total	Expenditures in 1947	
		Basic research	Applied research and development
Federal government	$ 625	$ 55	$ 570
Industry	450	10	440
University	45	35	10
Other	40	10	30
Total	$1,160	$110	$1,050

SOURCE: "Science and Public Policy," report by the President's Scientific Research Board, August, 1947, vol. I, p. 12.

to concrete and immediate problems. This was true even in the case of the atomic bomb." [26]

2. The Soviet Union's 1947 budget, for example, is reported to provide $1.2 billion for research and development. The Soviet national income is far smaller than ours, but its research and development expenditure is about equal to ours.[27]

3. Expenditure for research and development is probably about as high as it can effectively go, in view of present limitations upon our resources in trained manpower and facilities.[28]

4. As a nation, we devote far too small a proportion of our total income to research and development activities. Moreover, our expenditures are overly concentrated in applied research and development to the neglect of basic research. "The Nation could profitably devote more than 1 per cent (of the national income) to these purposes; it cannot safely spend less." [29] Our present expenditures amount to about one half of 1 per cent.

This report strongly suggests that the American economy does not generate the production of new technical ideas to the extent either possible or desirable. Its achievements in assimilating

[26] "Science and Public Policy," report by the President's Scientific Research Board, August, 1947, vol. I, pp. 4–5.
[27] *Ibid.*, pp. 5–6. [28] *Ibid.*, p. 13. [29] *Ibid.*, p. 26.

and putting to use the basic research findings of the entire world have been considerable. These achievements are not a substitute for the production of new ideas. With the decline in basic scientific research in Western Europe since World War II, the United States will be compelled to expand its pure research or suffer a slowdown in technological progress.

It is impossible to measure all aspects of economic progressiveness. Estimates of the rise in productivity—the extent to which methods of production become more efficient—can be made. However, the contribution to living standards from the creation of new products, which is no less important a type of progressiveness than changes in productivity, defies accurate measurement.

The rise in productivity of American industry between 1850 and 1940 has averaged 1.7 per cent a year,[30] but it varied widely among industrial sectors. In manufacturing the rise was between 3 and 3.5 per cent. In agriculture the rise was only 1.27 per cent. An annual increase in productivity of 1.7 per cent means that total output produced by a given number of working hours roughly doubles every forty years. (The annual rise must be "compounded.") Whereas certain economically backward countries have been able to increase productivity more rapidly than the United States, primarily by imitating our methods, no other developed industrial country has done better.

Thus, the United States economy has been progressive, despite its relatively small expenditures for research. Presumably it could easily have been even more progressive.

III. ACHIEVEMENTS OF THE AMERICAN ECONOMY

Our discussion of the economy of the United States thus far has been inconclusive. At every point we found no reliable criteria that could be applied to evaluate its performance; even where criteria did exist, data needed to apply them were lacking. As a result, the foregoing picture has primarily consisted of a listing of shortcomings and of achievements, and no balance between them was struck. Is there no way in which we can summarize the combined influence of all aspects of the present-day American economy?

[30] J. F. Dewhurst and Associates, *America's Needs and Resources* (New York: Twentieth Century Fund, 1947), pp. 22–23. See also *Monthly Labor Review*, Decembe 1946, pp. 893–917.

A] STANDARDS FOR JUDGING AN ECONOMY AS A WHOLE

Economic welfare is ordinarily measured by the output of an economy for each person that must be supported, giving due weight to the amount of effort involved in the production of output. This measure has important shortcomings, but it is the best available. Lacking a better indicator of an economy's performance, it will be used here. The reader is urged to recognize that vital elements of welfare are not reflected in measurements of output per person.

Personal experience indicates that the average American has far more goods and services than he had even fifteen years ago. And, looking back over a longer period, the standard of living in this country has soared. That it has increased greatly over long periods of time attests to the ability of our economy to improve living standards. Such evidence cannot be used to demonstrate that the economy is "efficient," however. *To judge the efficiency of anything requires a comparison of alternatives.* We must compare what was done under our system with what might have been achieved under another system. Such comparisons cannot be made easily. However, if we are to evaluate our economy, we must make them as best we can.

B] ADVANTAGES ENJOYED BY THE UNITED STATES

Two types of comparison might be made. The one most often made in the United States is that of absolute standards of living, that is, comparisons of the amount of goods possessed by each individual on the average in different countries. Overlooking the difficulties of comparing living standards in nations that consume different kinds of products, we must nevertheless ask whether differences in living standards are attributable entirely to differences in the efficiency of economic systems. Surely, if all conditions other than the economic system were everywhere the same, then differences in living standards could be attributed only to differences in economic systems. Nations, however, differ in many respects. The high living standards in the United States may be due to circumstances other than its economic system. While these circumstances may not fully account for our high living standards, it is difficult to doubt that they account for at least part of our economic superiority.

The United States enjoys the following advantages over most of the world's developed nations, and these advantages could possibly account for all or part of our high standard of living. First, the United States is well endowed with such natural gifts as rich deposits of raw materials, rivers for easy communication and transportation, excellent water-power sites, highly fertile soil, and a temperate climate. Second, the United States is free from the ravages and losses of war. While most other nations had to remain prepared against military aggression for more than a century, the United States maintained only insignificant token military forces. During the last two world wars, many nations in the world were heavily damaged by direct military conflict; the United States, on the other hand, greatly expanded its industrial resources during those wars. Combat losses, generally concentrated among the cream of a population, were a far smaller percentage of our population in World Wars I and II than they were in the other belligerent nations. Third, most Americans are descendants of those venturesome and intelligent persons who saw in emigration a chance for advancement. These persons risked a dangerous and acutely uncomfortable voyage to these shores; many of them undertook a hazardous journey within the United States to a dangerous frontier; many assimilated an unfamiliar language and culture. Those who survived these ordeals probably formed a more hardy and industrious population than was to be found in most other nations. Fourth, the large number of immigrants that settled in the United States, especially up to World War I, represented an important economic gain, resulting from the fact that many millions of immigrants were reared at the expense of other countries and came to the United States only after they were economically productive. These four advantages are surely not trifling. However, their precise importance cannot be measured.

C] AMERICAN LEVELS OF LIVING COMPARED WITH THOSE OF OTHER NATIONS

Whatever the causes of differences in living levels of various countries, Table 2-6 presents the best available indicator of the differences that do exist. According to these data, the United States enjoys by far the highest level of living in the world.

Few people question that the American level of living is the highest, but many might doubt that the margin of superiority is as great as indicated in the table. There are great difficulties in comparing living conditions in different countries, some of which cannot be fully overcome. Such comparisons, therefore, must be considered only rough approximations.

It would appear that Table 2-6 exaggerates the margin of superiority of American living levels over those in other countries. Some foreign economists who have lived in the United States for some time insist that the difference between living conditions in their native lands and in the United States is far smaller than the statistics in Table 2-6 would suggest.

The salient fact nevertheless remains that the American economy does provide the highest per capita output of material goods. Moreover, this large output does not arise from very long hours of work or the employment of large numbers of women and young and aged persons. The American economy is unquestionably the most productive in the world.

D] SUMMARY EVALUATION OF THE AMERICAN ECONOMIC SYSTEM

In evaluating American capitalism, we are hampered by two factors. First, we lack reliable criteria—at least criteria that can be applied directly—by which the economy's performance can be judged. Second, much of the evidence that might be collected to help evaluate our economy is lacking. Consequently, whatever judgments we reach are, at best, only carefully reasoned guesses resting on slender evidence.

The lack of reliable criteria by which economic performance can be judged is itself a major weakness of our economy. If we have no accurate measure of the best goods to produce, the best jobs in which a man should work, the best methods of production to utilize, and the most suitable manner to distribute income, *how can we expect to perform those basic economic functions efficiently?* A vital element in any economy is a workable standard, yardstick, or unit of account that permits accurate comparisons of the worth of goods, the importance of particular positions, and the efficiency of particular productive techniques. While money values of goods, costs of services, and wage rates are the best indicators that exist in our economy, they clearly are defective. As a result, we cannot, except by accident, help make mistakes—they could be large and important mistakes—in the way we use our resources.

Individuals can, and indeed they do, violently disagree about

TABLE 2-6

Seventy Countries Classified by Size of Per Capita Income in 1949 and Broad Continental Division
(In United States dollars)

Per capita income	Africa	Asia	Europe	Central America	South America	Australasia
Under $50	Ethiopia Liberia	Burma China Indonesia South Korea Philippines Saudi Arabia Thailand Yemen		Haiti	Ecuador	
$50–$100		Afghanistan Ceylon India Iran Iraq Pakistan		Dominican Republic Guatemala Honduras Nicaragua	Bolivia El Salvador Paraguay	
$100–$200	Egypt Southern Rhodesia	Japan Lebanon Syria Turkey	Greece Yugoslavia	Costa Rica Mexico Panama	Brazil Chile Colombia Peru	

Per capita income	Africa	Asia	Europe	North and Central America	South America	Australasia
$200–$300	Union of South Africa		Austria Hungary Italy Portugal	Cuba		
$300–$400		Israel	Czecho-slovakia Finland Germany Poland U.S.S.R.		Argentina Uruguay Venezuela	
$400–$600			Belgium France Iceland Ireland Luxembourg Netherlands Norway			
$600–$900			Denmark Sweden Switzerland United Kingdom	Canada United States		Australia New Zealand

SOURCE: Adapted from *National and Per Capita Incomes, Seventy Countries, 1949* (New York: Statistical Office of the United Nations, 1950), p. 28.

the importance of individual defects in the present American economy. Lacking reliable measures of performance, these disagreements cannot be resolved. There cannot be any disagreement, however, about the necessity of providing some reliable measure of performance—whether it be altogether new or simply an improvement in the indicator we now use. Imperfect as our criteria for judgment are and even though only limited evidence exists on many points, it is clear that our economy is very productive. It is equally clear that considerable opportunity for improvement exists.

Most of the failures of the American economy to achieve the ultimate in efficiency can be attributed to two shortcomings. First, competition both among businesses in the sale of goods and services and among workers and lenders in the provision of productive factors frequently is not keen. That is, by accident, tradition, or by carefully constructed arrangements, the rivalry among individuals and businesses is blunted. Therefore, some businessmen feel no irresistible pressure to produce the things that consumers want. Their market position sometimes is so strong that they can compel the consumer to accept whatever they choose to offer him. Similarly, due to the weakness or absence of competition, some businessmen are not compelled to use the most productive methods available and are not even forced to keep abreast of technological developments. Occasionally by superior efficiency, but no less often by cooperation or collusion or by the use of rough-and-ready market practices, some firms have grown to huge proportions. They are able to treat their suppliers, labor, and distributors with relatively little regard for the consequences. Many other shortcomings of the economic system outlined above can be traced primarily to an absence of keen competition.

As a rough rule, the price system and capitalism is efficient to the extent that rivalry is unrestrained—save in ways in which the public might be injured. This rule can be derived directly from the rationale underlying the American economy. It makes sense only to the extent that keen rivalry operates in markets for the sale of goods and services. To a considerable, but not accurately measurable, extent, American product and labor markets are shot through with monopolistic arrangements and with conventional methods of doing business that represent serious departures from unbridled competition.

The second major shortcoming of the American economic system, already mentioned but deserving greater emphasis, is its instability. The susceptibility of the American economy to business cycles—depressions primarily, but also inflations—is possibly its greatest defect. Various defects of the American economy beyond the obvious direct waste of manpower through idleness can be traced to economic instability. Business cycles color the attitudes of businessmen, for example, and discourage investment that might substantially improve the efficiency of production. Individuals are compelled to accept almost any type of employment during depression and may for a variety of reasons fail to shift to occupations in which they would be more productive. Persons who are capable of acquiring the highest type of skill may be compelled to accept employment as unskilled workers because they reached maturity during a depression and their parents were unable to finance added training for them. In these and many other ways, business cycles prevent the American economy from realizing its full potential efficiency.

It must be emphasized that all other known economic systems also fail to unleash the full productive efforts of individuals and business organizations. They too, therefore, suffer from the equivalent of imperfect competition. Economic instability, however, seems more characteristic of the United States than of the Soviet Union and the United Kingdom. This defect, however, is not inherent in the capitalistic system itself and seems amenable to correction. Virtually every elementary economics textbook describes a variety of measures by which cyclical fluctuations could be checked. Moreover, these measures are altogether consistent with the underlying rationale and principles of a free enterprise economy.

IV. NONECONOMIC EFFECTS OF CAPITALISM

Americans usually judge a foreign economy by its noneconomic as well as its economic characteristics. In evaluating the Soviet Union, for example, among the first things mentioned by Americans is its undemocratic character. By democracy we designate a political rather than an economic condition. Other criticisms frequently made of the Soviet Union are that it uses forced labor camps and that it infringes upon religious liberty. These conditions also are essentially noneconomic.

Even as the Soviet economic system is held accountable for certain political and social conditions, so, too, *capitalism seems responsible for many of the social and political conditions that prevail in the United States.* A full evaluation of an economic system therefore requires consideration of the noneconomic circumstances to which it gives rise.

Unfortunately, one cannot determine reliably how much of the political, social, and attitudinal environment in any country results from the characteristics of its economic system and how much is due to other causes. Present arrangements grow out of past conditions. Even after a violent revolution, a nation does not change its entire character. Communist sympathizers, for example, assert that the objectionable characteristics of Soviet communism are due to the Russian heritage of dictatorship, absence of civil liberties, and the habitual use of harsh and brutal methods by the authorities.

Countries with ostensibly the same economic system (namely, the United States, the United Kingdom, Belgium, France, and Germany during the 1920's) differed significantly in their noneconomic characteristics. Clearly, the economic system alone cannot be held responsible for all political, social, and attitudinal circumstances. In the discussion that follows, only those features of the United States that might be attributed to its economic system will be considered.

The noneconomic effects of capitalism will be discussed under three heads: the effect of capitalism on the predominant attitudes; the political effects of capitalism; and the social and psychological effects of capitalism. Little space is accorded to these subjects, because the author is an economist and intended this book to deal primarily with economic matters.

A] THE EFFECT OF CAPITALISM ON THE PREDOMINANT ATTITUDES

Perhaps the most serious indictment against capitalism concerns its effect on personal attitudes. Some people maintain that, while capitalism in the United States has provided a relatively large output of goods, it has also produced attitudes that make us dissatisfied and unhappy. The attitudes attributed to capitalism that are said to result in general dissatisfaction among Americans can be grouped under the heading of "materialism." Materialism is an outlook on life that puts a high premium on the acquisition, possession, and use of material objects of wealth. It thereby weakens personal spiritual values and any desire to perform community service. Materialism contributes no philosophy that provides a satisfying purpose to life nor does it help individuals to adjust happily. It weakens the influence of religious teachings without offering any satisfying alternative.

Capitalism, however, can be credited with a major contribution to a happy outlook by making most people believe they possess great and almost equal opportunities to advance themselves and can succeed if only they try. This attitude gives people hope and also flatters them into a feeling of basic equality and personal dignity. It also probably encourages people to make more strenuous efforts to improve themselves than they might otherwise make, and they probably gain lasting satisfaction from the achievements that result from their efforts.

As in the discussion of other noneconomic consequences of capitalism (and of the other systems studied), materialism under capitalism will not receive full discussion. The small space allotted to these points does not imply that they are unimportant or that they are so universally acknowledged that they require no discussion. Instead, they should be regarded as allegations that seem to possess sufficient merit to deserve careful consideration.

B] POLITICAL EFFECTS OF CAPITALISM

One of the major noneconomic claims for capitalism is that it results in political democracy. Where capitalism has prevailed, ordinarily most people have had equal voting power. Partial offsets against this major claim for capitalism are to be found in the charge that capitalism mars the quality of democracy in several ways. First, disproportionate political power is exerted by those who control large economic resources. Second, the electorate is apathetic and badly informed.[31] Third, political power is exerted primarily by

---

[31] An indication of public apathy and misinformation about public issues generally is obtained as a by-product of public opinion polls. When people's opinions are asked about some public issue or personality, the pollsters also learn how many were never aware of the issue or never heard of the person.

The *Public Opinion Quarterly* carries in each issue a compilation of all available results of polls in the United States based on a national cross section. This topically arranged summary is among the most interesting and illuminating sources of information one can hope to read. A few issues of the magazine turned up the following evidence of lack of information on the part of citizens.

1. As of December, 1948, 21% never heard or read about the civil war in China.

groups organized along economic lines, and these groups pursue policies which restrict rather than enlarge output.

In assessing the political effects of capitalism, primarily one wants to know if capitalism in the United States has resulted in a government that represents the true interests of the people and responds to their wishes as well as another equally productive economic system might. We cannot assume that only capitalism results in democracy or that only capitalism fails to realize fully the benefits of democracy.

C] SOCIAL AND PSYCHOLOGICAL EFFECTS OF CAPITALISM

Capitalism over most of the world generally and in the United States particularly has been associated with minimum restraint on occupational choice, personal expression, and in free choice of a "way of life." Psychologists are agreed that the absence of restraint contributes to healthy mental balance, personal happiness, and to successful social adjustment.

There are, however, social and psychological effects of capitalism that are not to its credit. These will simply be listed without discussion. First, most people in the United States live under heavy nervous pressure; they feel insecure and believe current prosperity can quickly be turned into pauperism; that one can be fired from his good job "out of the blue" without much cause. Second, employees are subject to the arbitrary power of their employer; in this sense, no worker is completely free. Employers have, in addition to their power to fire, the ability to injure employees by giving poor references to other potential employers. (Strong unions check the employer's power but sometimes create another arbitrary power over the individual worker.) Capitalism makes of the pursuit of

---

2. A poll on January 30, 1949, showed that 36% never heard or read about the House Un-American Activities Committee.

3. The Marshall Plan, however designated, evoked a negative response from 18% of those polled.

(The preceding examples came from the spring, 1949, issue.)

4. Of the people polled on April 1, 1949, 44% had not heard or read about the Truman administration's plan for compulsory health insurance.

5. Polled about the amount people pay in federal income taxes on three different incomes, respondents were very wide of the mark on two (summer, 1949).

6. Of those questioned, 55% did not know about the "Voice of America Broadcasts" (fall, 1949).

7. On December 22, 1950, 34% could not correctly identify Dean Acheson (spring, 1951).

8. The initials F.B.I. had no meaning for 16% of those polled (winter, 1949–1950).

money the highest goal and the most engrossing activity. It often creates a conflict between family obligations and business success.

V. CONCLUSIONS

The foregoing description and evaluation of American capitalism is admittedly sketchy and superficial. To describe and evaluate an economic system is immensely complicated. This chapter has done little more than raise the major questions that must be answered before we understand our own economy.

Doubts have been expressed about the extent to which the rationale for capitalism applies to the present economic system in the United States. Many criticisms of the American economy have been made. However, capitalism has been evaluated here by absolute standards. When a condition has been criticized, it does not follow that other types of economy excel in that respect. Conditions termed defects call for improvement, but measures for improvement may not exist and may never be devised. Some defects, however, can surely be remedied. Need for intensive research into the performance of our economy and the means for its improvement is manifest. At present, economic research is disorganized. Awareness of the existence of many defects that might be remedied should inspire us to make greater expenditures toward understanding the workings of our economy. Social scientists must be made to feel a responsibility for devising and vigorously advocating measures that will correct these defects. Moveover, the average voter must be prepared to take a more active interest in politics if significant improvements are to be made.

CHAPTER THREE

The Economy of the Soviet Union

The discussion of the economy of the Soviet Union differs in important particulars from that of the American economy. The preceding chapter dealt with something that is generally familiar; the Soviet economy, on the other hand, is a complete mystery to most people. The Soviet authorities admittedly try to keep most economic information about their country from the rest of the world; hence even after all the available data are assembled, the picture is vague and incomplete. As a result, major attention will be devoted to describing to the best of our knowledge how the Soviet economy operates, and relatively little space will be given to critical evaluation, since what is not known can scarcely be evaluated. In this very important respect, the American and the Soviet economies are not treated in a parallel manner.

Indeed, the purposes of this and the preceding chapter are different. In the discussion of the United States, standards by which an economy might be evaluated were set forth and applied to the American economy in an effort to discover whether it performs as effectively as it might. The purpose was essentially critical, for it was hoped that this approach would reveal areas in which economic operations could be improved. In studying the Soviet economy, our interest in improving its operations is slight at best. Primarily, we want to know how it works, and what leads the Soviet leaders to believe that it works better than other types of economic system. By studying the Soviet economy with this purpose in view, we hope to learn something of value in the conduct of our own economic activities. For these reasons, the Soviet economy receives less detailed criticism than was advanced for the American economy. To prevent a possible erroneous impression, the reader should know at the outset that the author believes the existing American economic system to be more efficient and its noneconomic consequences more favorable than a system of detailed economic planning based on the Soviet model would be in this country.

I. APPROACHES TO A STUDY OF THE SOVIET UNION

The Union of Soviet Socialist Republics (hereinafter called the Soviet Union) may be studied with four major ends in view. They are to review its accomplishments, to understand the manner in which the economy functions, to explain the manner in which the economy developed to its present condition, and finally to understand its likely future development. Each of these possible approaches may be undertaken separately.

By a review of the accomplishments of the Soviet Union, we mean essentially a description of what was and what was not achieved since the new economic system was initiated. Pursuit of this goal calls primarily for a review of the nation's production performance. To review the accomplishments of the Soviet Union, there is no need to understand how it functions, but only to observe its results, without respect to the economic arrangements by which they were achieved.

To comprehend how the economy of the Soviet Union functions is far more complicated than to review its achievements. It is necessary to describe Soviet procedures and institutional arrangements and to analyze their functioning with the purpose of understanding how the economy works so that one could, if he had to do so, set up an economy like that of the Soviet Union. One can understand how the Soviet economy operates without knowing its achievements.

Many persons study the Soviet Union in an effort to understand why Marxists first gained control in that country and how the economy developed to its present form. This method of approach analyzes the step-by-step development of the economy and is fundamentally historical.

Finally, some people concentrate upon those aspects of the Soviet Union which suggest the direction in which the economy will develop in the future. Since the Soviet Union has become one of the two leading military powers in the world, the probable future course of its development is a matter of great moment to Americans.

The fundamental purpose of the following discussion is to explain the functioning of the Soviet economy, with special emphasis on its unique features. More particularly, the aim is to make clear the manner in which a planned economy (of the Soviet type) solves the basic economic problems of deciding what to produce, how much to produce, by what means to produce, how to get people into the "right jobs," how to distribute income, and how to make the economy progressive. When that undertaking has been completed, the accomplishments of the Soviet Union under its economic system of detailed economic planning will be reviewed briefly. The following discussion is not organized along historical lines and does not probe into probable future developments.

II. DISTINGUISHING FEATURES OF THE SOVIET ECONOMY

It will be impossible to describe the economy of the Soviet Union in full detail. Fundamentally, it is similar to our own economy in that most of the population work under the supervision and direction of others to produce goods and services. Although an attempt will be made to show how the major parts of the Soviet economy fit together, the description must remain sketchy, the emphasis being primarily upon the features of the economy that are very different from our own. These differences will be discussed under the heads of principles underlying the Soviet economy, structural differences, and differences in function.

A] PRINCIPLES UNDERLYING THE SOVIET ECONOMY

The Soviet Union is guided by the principle that the economy should be directed toward socially prescribed goals, and that planners should devise the best measures possible within the law to achieve them. By "socially prescribed goals" is meant objectives set down for the nation as a whole. These goals are specified in concrete terms by the political authorities and may reflect a wide variety of considerations—cultural, social, political, military, and so on. These goals are decided "arbitrarily" by individuals, inasmuch as they are conscious choices among alternatives and could have been decided differently.

"Prescribed goals" are perhaps clearest when contrasted with the goals of our own economy. In the United States, the output goals of the economy—let alone such matters as the number of teachers to be trained, the number of hospitals to be built, and so on—are not centrally determined. They just happen as the result of decisions made by many persons operating more or less independently.[1] In the Soviet Union virtually all matters relating to the use of economic resources (including personal services in research, the arts, training in the colleges and technical schools, and the like) are determined by a central group whose major function is to decide such matters.

As indicated, in the Soviet Union the authorities are free to use virtually any means they may devise to attain the prescribed goals. They face two major prohibitions. First, no one may "profit"—that is, obtain money income—from the employment of others or from the purchase and resale of goods. Second, no private ownership of the *means of production* is allowed. (As we shall see, a notable exception exists in the form of private plots of land on collective farms; virtually all consumers' goods are privately owned in the Soviet Union.)

In addition, the authorities are constrained to some degree by an extensive body of doctrine composed of the writings of Marx, Engels, Lenin, and Stalin. While the Russians have shown considerable flexibility in interpreting the words of the leading Communist writers, and in some cases have flatly rejected policies that were stated by Marx and Engels,[2] unquestionably Marxian theory influences the means used in the Soviet Union to achieve the prescribed goals. Space limitations prohibit a discussion of Communist doctrine.

To understand the Soviet Union requires, perhaps above all else, knowledge of the goals pursued by its leaders. To explain most people and arrangements, the best clue is their fundamental purposes and objectives. In the case of the Soviet Union, we must ask what those persons who exert dominant control over the nation want to achieve both for themselves and for the nation as a whole. To answer these questions requires an exploration of the Soviet political system to determine what persons possess dominant power. Then

---

[1] The resemblance between the United States and the Soviet Union is closest in military matters. The American output of military goods, in total value, is determined centrally by Congress. The responsible military authorities decide what specific goods shall be produced. Similarly, during wartime or a large defense program, a substantial degree of central economic planning is employed.

[2] For example, Marx's position on the use of money and Engels' views on specialization in a socialistic society were not adopted by the Soviet Union either in principle or in practice. See H. Schwartz, *Russia's Soviet Economy* (New York: Prentice-Hall, Inc., 1950), pp. 84–85.

we must examine and speculate on the motives of those persons. Before the end of this discussion of the Soviet Union, we shall consider its political system and locus of power at the present time. At this point, it should suffice to state that, in the author's opinion, the Soviet Union is a firm dictatorship (whether of one man or a small group he is not sure) and that the political power is lodged in the Presidium of the Central Committee of the Communist Party formerly known as the Politburo. The goals *stated* by the best political authorities fall under the head of creating a socialist society, and include the following:

1. An expansion of the industrial productive capacity of the nation. This expansion is sought as a base for a rapidly increasing standard of living and as a foundation for military power, which the leaders state they desire for defensive purposes.
2. An improvement in literacy and a raising of cultural levels.
3. Improvement in national health standards.
4. Elimination of political, economic, and psychological insecurity.

Whatever their real purposes, the Soviet leaders say that they do not seek expanded territories, and they do not claim to be members of a superior race. Their *stated* objectives are similar to those of Western European countries and the United States. They are almost complete opposites of those of Nazi Germany and Fascist Italy. They pay frequent and elaborate compliments to the virtues of democracy. They demand the participation of all persons in matters pertaining to their jobs and their community. Moreover, most of these principles are explicitly incorporated in the constitution of the Soviet Union. The actual behavior of the Soviet leaders and the real conditions there differ significantly from those in Nazi Germany and Fascist Italy.[3] However, they also differ substantially from the stated goals and principles.

The objectives attributed to the leaders of the Soviet Union by its sternest critics include the following: to retain their political power as long as possible by whatever means are necessary; to exploit the people they govern to obtain luxuries for themselves; to impose their will upon the rest of the world in order to expand their power; and to spread Communism and eliminate the threat to it that comes from the non-Communist world.

[3] For a discerning comparison of the dictatorship in the Soviet Union and the dictatorships of Hitler and Mussolini, see J. Towster, *Political Power in the U.S.S.R. 1917–1947* (New York: Oxford University Press, 1948), pp. 390–394.

Certainly it is dangerous to judge people's motives solely by the things they say. What they say, however, should not be ignored entirely. The Soviet rulers may be tyrannical, cruel, hard, shrewd, and power-hungry men. They must nevertheless be distinguished from politically powerful men in non-Communist nations. Those who rule the Soviet Union have doubtless been strongly influenced by the doctrines they learned and preached before and during the Communist Revolution. They are likely to have absorbed and accepted most of the views espoused by Marx, Engels, and Lenin. Therefore, their motives are to be understood in considerable measure by understanding Communist doctrine.

These men unquestionably hold many views and personal objectives that are not covered by Marxian theory one way or another. They may not accept Marxian doctrine in totality. One would suppose that they are motivated in some measure by such purely personal goals as the attainment of high office, the desire to help members of their family and close friends, a wish to lead a comfortable and secure life, and the like. However, in the absence of evidence to the contrary, it is safest to assume that the persons exercising the political power in the Soviet Union believe in the writings of Marx, Engels, and Lenin and are under great pressure to make their actions consistent with the Marxian doctrines. Deviations from those doctrines are certain to arouse criticism in many quarters. However, at least one man, Josef Stalin, seems to be completely safe from criticism.

To fathom the true motives and intentions of the Soviet rulers is one of the foremost tasks of our times. The key to Stalin's mind will not be found here, however. To study the Soviet economy, it is not necessary to explore the objectives of the Soviet leaders further.[4] No matter what their most fundamental aims, there is no reason why they would desire to produce few goods rather than many, and why they would prefer to work long hours if they could produce as much in less time. *Accordingly, we can safely assume that the paramount economic objective of the Soviet leaders is to increase the output of goods and services as rapidly as possible with a minimum of sacrifice.*

To sum up, let us crystallize the difference in principles under-

[4] The motives of the political leaders of the Soviet Union are relevant in some measure even to the study of the economy, for they determine what basic objectives will be pursued. However, we shall only explore the extent to which the economy successfully achieves whatever objectives it pursues.

lying the Soviet and the American economic systems. In the United States, everyone may do whatever he wishes within the law, and it is expected that the outcome will be better than could be obtained from any other method of organizing our economy. The goals of the economy are not specified; we simply accept whatever happens as a result of the fact that all individuals independently pursue their own personal objectives. The Russians state very specifically what they want to happen and then take the best measures they can devise to achieve their goals.

B] STRUCTURAL DIFFERENCES BETWEEN THE AMERICAN AND SOVIET ECONOMIES

For the most part, the Soviet Union employs economic institutions that are also used in the United States. However, the great bulk of all industrial output is produced in establishments owned by the state. These enterprises are not significantly different in form from the TVA, the Post Office, and locally owned public utilities in the United States. An important type of industrial enterprise is the producers' cooperative (also known as "industrial cooperatives" and "handicraftsmen's cooperatives") which is similar in structure to consumer and agricultural cooperatives in the United States.

In agriculture, the Soviet Union does employ a unique arrangement known as the collective farm. Collective farms may be regarded as a combination of simple cooperative and private enterprise. Each family on a collective farm is given a plot of land with which it may do whatever it wishes, but most of its efforts must be devoted to working the lands belonging to all members of the collective farm in common. A family's income depends primarily upon its share in the collective farm's total output. Members of collective farms do not share equally; their shares vary according to the amount and type of work done for the farm.

The collective farm is a compromise between Communist principles and political expediency. The farm population in Russia did not actively support the Communist Party and, at least according to Communist doctrine, is ordinarily a source of reaction hostile to the Communists. Accordingly, the farmers represented the greatest potential source of effective political opposition to the Communists. The magnitude of this threat can be appreciated only when it is recalled that about 80 per cent of the total Russian population was agrarian at the time of the Revolution. The Soviet leaders, apparently fearful that overspeedy socialization of agriculture would alienate the independent, nonpolitically enlightened (by their standards) peasant, devised this compromise. From a political point of view, the collectivization of agriculture represented a great achievement by the regime—though one for which the nation paid heavily in human misery and lives.

In addition to collective farms, which account for 91 per cent of the total cultivated area of the country,[5] state farms are used in the Soviet Union to produce over 8 per cent of total agricultural output and to pioneer in the development of new agricultural methods. State farms are analogous to state-owned industrial enterprises. Every person engaged on a state farm is simply an employee of the farm; his income depends completely upon his salary; he does not share in the proceeds of the farm, and thus is spared the risks to which the collective farmer is exposed.

The Soviet Union uses money as a medium of exchange—that is, the government has created a convenient medium that is universally acceptable in exchange. Money also serves as a "unit of account"—that is, production costs, the government budget, and the like are calculated in money terms even as in the United States. Similarly, the Soviet Union uses banks, and even charges interest for most loans.

The Soviet banks, however, differ from those in the United States in that they are a vital part of the planning machinery. They serve as a strategic source of information that permits the planning authorities to uncover deviations from the economic plan. Thus, the Soviet banks, while performing the same functions as our banks, also serve as an arm of the planning authorities. Their function in this connection will be discussed further at a later point.

The Soviet Union has employment exchanges and labor unions and the equivalent of social security laws. Since the nation is a "Workers' State," the arrangements pertaining to labor, while nominally similar to those in the United States, are also different in significant respects. When we come to a discussion of the role of the worker in the Soviet Union, these differences will be made clear. At this point, we should note that similar arrangements and institutions affecting labor exist in the United States and in the Soviet Union.

Advertising, a practice heavily attacked by Communists in capitalist countries, is employed and even highly praised in the

---

[5] W. N. Loucks and J. W. Hoot, *Comparative Economic Systems* (New York: Harper & Brothers, 1948), p. 485.

Soviet Union.[6] As indicated, the Soviet Union also allows private ownership of most consumers' goods and relies heavily on monetary incentives to secure maximum productive effort.

The vital difference between the United States and the Soviet Union is not to be found in their institutions—that is, in their economic structure, as the word is employed here—but in the way those institutions operate. That difference consists in the presence of detailed planning machinery in the Soviet Union and its absence in the United States. Put differently, in the Soviet Union, central authorities prescribe the goals of the economy and dictate the means by which they are to be pursued.

C] FUNCTIONAL DIFFERENCES BETWEEN THE AMERICAN AND SOVIET ECONOMIES

The American, British, and Soviet economies differ fundamentally in the degree to which economic decisions are made centrally and "arbitrarily." In the Soviet Union, only relatively minor economic decisions are made by persons other than the planners. Decisions about the quantity of goods to be made, the quality of product to be turned out, the location at which goods are to be made, and the methods to employ in production are made by central agencies with reference to a single central plan that is drawn up to knit the entire economy together.

Subordination of the economy to a single economic plan is not peculiar to the Soviet Union. The United Kingdom has something that represents an over-all plan for the entire economy in the form of its annual "White Papers." France had its "Monnet Plan," and most Scandinavian countries also set up general economic goals for the economy. *What is unique about the Soviet Union is the enormous detail of the centralized plan, the rigor of the measures taken to realize its goals, and the extent to which the economic plan takes precedence over and dominates all individual economic decisions in the nation.*

Accordingly, a description of the structure of the Soviet economy will not give much insight into its essential character. *To understand the Soviet economy requires, above all, knowledge of the goals of the Soviet leaders and of the techniques of planning that are employed.* We will understand the Soviet economy only if we know how the plans are drawn up, how records are kept of progress

[6] *New York Herald Tribune,* December 3, 1950.

under their plans, how and when plans are modified, the kinds of action taken when experience departs significantly from the plan, and the types of data on which their plans rest. The Soviet economy is a system of highly detailed economic planning, and in this respect it is unique. We shall turn now to a description of planning in the Soviet Union.

III. HOW DETAILED ECONOMIC PLANNING IS CONDUCTED IN THE SOVIET UNION

From the time the present group took power in the Soviet Union, it prepared for extensive planning of the economy. Before the present highly detailed form of planning was attained, the Soviet economy relied on very simple plans that affected only one or a few branches of industry.[7] (The first plan, known as the Goelro, was adopted in 1921 and was concerned almost exclusively with electric power generating capacity.) The fourth five-year plan, adopted in 1945, was extremely detailed, and set output goals for literally hundreds of products. The fifth was announced on August 21, 1952.

The long-range plans in the Soviet Union have been mostly for five-year periods, though plans for longer and shorter duration have also been made. Economic change is more gradual than is implied by a succession of five-year plans. The Soviet economy does not take sudden and drastic turns every five years. Each enterprise is governed by plans of short duration, typically for three months or less. Presumably these short-period plans call for only gradual changes from the past, except in extreme emergency.

Before the mechanics of planning in the Soviet Union are outlined, two general points should be recognized. First, if one conceives of planning as the formulation of plans "from scratch" by which the activities of all individuals and plants are directed, it will surely appear impossible. In practice, planners are able to build on the present and the past. Planning primarily takes the form of projecting changes from the present. That is, planners decide in what ways existing arrangements might be improved; they do not draw up a completely different set of arrangements. Second, plans

[7] For a description of the gradual development of planning in the Soviet Union, see A. Baykov, *The Development of the Soviet Economic System* (New York: The Macmillan Company, 1947), pp. 423–444; and A. Kursky, *The Planning of the National Economy of the USSR* (Moscow: Foreign Languages Publishing House, 1949), pp. 120–216.

are not made "once and for all." If it turns out that something is out of kilter, a correction will be made.

By patching up mistakes in the original plan, the planners may end up with an efficient plan. Once they have achieved an efficient arrangement of the various parts of the economy, it should not be very difficult to maintain efficiency even while some modifications are made in the economy. However, during the period when the economy is undergoing basic changes—such as a large relocation of industry, a sharp shift in the rate of capital formation, and the like —then correction of mistakes would not be easy and would not insure efficiency. On the other hand, even such basic changes would not require replanning from the ground up. *The ability to build on the past and to change things around if plans are out of line enormously simplifies the task of planning.* Indeed, without it, efficient planning would almost certainly be impossible.

A] WHY ECONOMIC PLANNING IS SO COMPLICATED

Why has the very possibility of efficient economic planning been called into question? Essentially, it is contended that so many factors should enter into the decisions about what, how much, and how to produce that human beings are incapable of deciding these matters correctly. Moreover, it can be argued that, even if these decisions could somehow be made correctly, they would require so much time that the plans would always be out of date, and the labors of so many people would be required that little could be produced besides economic plans.

1. *Characteristics of a Good Economic Plan*

A good economic plan calls for the production of goods in accordance with the preference of consumers for products and in accordance with the occupational choices of productive factors.[8] That is, things of equal "cost" should be produced solely on the basis of consumer choice; goods equally desired by consumers should be produced according to the relative willingness of productive factors to produce them. Put more simply, a good plan would respect the desires both of consumers and of productive factors. But how can one obtain full and reliable information about the desires of consumers and of productive factors? We shall see presently that some infor-

[8] At times other considerations override these. However, these are by far the most important in the ordinary case.

mation does exist and is used in the Soviet Union, but it is neither easy to obtain nor simple to interpret.

In addition to the enormous difficulty of determining the relative importance of various products, and the attitude of workers toward different kinds of work, planners face extremely complicated "technical" problems in drawing up a good plan. Plans must be kept in balance. There are several types of balance that must be maintained if the general economic plan is to be efficient. Certain balances will be termed "crosswise" balances; others will be called "backward" balances. An explanation of these types of balance will help to make clear why economic planning is so complicated.

A] Crosswise Balances. Certain relationships must be maintained between various economic circumstances. First, output goals set by an economic plan should require the use of all available productive factors—no more and no less. To call for less output than the available labor force could produce would result in underemployment—a mark of inefficient planning. To call for more output than the available manpower could turn out would necessarily result in failure to produce all that had been planned, and might lead to unavoidable interruptions in production.

The crosswise balance between all output goals and the total available manpower should also hold for other productive factors, such as power, transportation, and the basic metals. All that is available should be fully used and the plans should not call for more than is available. It would be difficult enough to plan output so that exactly the available labor force would be used. But to use the labor force exactly and also use exactly the supply of power, transportation, basic metals, and the like is vastly more complicated. Evidence suggests that Soviet planners check crosswise balances of this type for over a hundred raw materials.

Another crosswise balance that must be maintained arises from the fact that production takes place in space. Planners must decide where output is to be produced. They must locate production with respect to the availability of manpower and with regard to the costs of transporting raw materials to the site of production. Consequently, an economic plan must have geographical balance—with the output goals for each area calling for the supplies of factors that are, or could easily be made, available in the area.

Still another crosswise balance that must be achieved by economic planners is that between physical conditions and financial conditions. In the Soviet Union, money is used to facilitate almost all economic activities. Workers are paid in money and they purchase goods with money. It is necessary, if the economy is to avoid inflation or an accumulation of inventories (which would result if the amount of money spent by consumers was far less than the prices of goods and services offered for sale), that money payments to individuals be kept in balance with prices charged. While the consequences of excessive and insufficient expenditure differ in planned and unplanned economies, they are undesirable in both. A perfect plan maintains an exact balance.

B] Backward Balances. Backward balances are relationships between the output of finished products and their components. For example, the output of automobile wheels and tires must be kept in line with the output of automobiles. If almost complete cars were to remain unusable for lack of wheels, or if far more wheels were produced than were needed, the plan would be out of balance and resources would have been used inefficiently.

A mere statement of the balances that must be maintained in a perfect plan shows that "perfect" plans are virtually impossible. It does not follow, however, that efficient planning is impossible or that planning is undesirable. Every economy falls far short of perfection. How efficient has detailed economic planning been in the Soviet Union?

B] THE PREPARATION OF A FIVE-YEAR PLAN IN THE SOVIET UNION [9]

The five-year plan is the spine of the Soviet economic system. While changes in circumstances will compel deviations from the plan, in the usual circumstances the plan directly and indirectly dictates what all enterprises in the Soviet Union are to do.

Five-year plans set down detailed specific tasks for many industries, and for all parts of the economy they set forth the most important goals that are to be pursued. All efforts to fulfill the plan are centered on these main goals, which are called "leading links." In the event it becomes impossible to meet all aims, the leading links are protected at the expense of other activities.

The relation between the five-year plans and the shorter plans is in dispute. This author believes, with most writers on the subject, that the one-year plans and plans of even shorter duration are vir-

[9] See particularly Kursky, *op. cit.*, and Schwartz, *op. cit.*, Chap. IV.

tually dictated by the provisions of the five-year plan, and simply
detailed expressions of the five-year plans adjusted to take accoun
of unforeseen developments. It has been argued that the five-year plans are prepared primarily for propaganda purposes and that the annual plans really direct the operations of the economy.[10]

The preparation of five-year plans can be divided into four stages. In the first stage, the highest political authorities set down general directives that indicate the basic goals to be pursued. That is, before any decisions about individual products are made, the objectives aimed for are decided upon. The second stage calls for the drawing up of detailed steps that must be taken in order to achieve the general objectives. Specifically, in this stage, output goals are set for most industries. The third stage is the adoption of the detailed plans. Finally, the execution of the plans is supervised to insure their fulfillment as far as possible.

1. *The First Stage: The Formulation of General Objectives*

The broad directives underlying five-year plans involve a variety of social, political, military, and diplomatic considerations. They deal with such matters as the proportion of resources to be devoted to investment in new facilities and to military purposes, the speed at which various regions are to be developed, the degree of dependence upon imports, and the like. The directives for the five-year plans are not simply wishes for the future; they must be internally consistent principles and objectives, based upon an understanding of how much the economy can produce.

These basic directives are set down officially by the Council of Ministers, but they originate with the top political authorities. Probably these are formulated by the Politburo, which is the executive committee of the Communist Party, not itself a regular organ of the Soviet government.

Most of a five-year plan spells out the broad directives. The preparation of detailed plans is what most people regard as economic planning, but the determination of the broad goals of the economy is perhaps the most vital step in the planning process. Broad directives determine the direction in which the economy will be steered. Detailed plans determine how quickly and efficiently the economy will move in that direction.

---

[10] David Granick, *Plant Management in the Soviet Industrial System,* dissertation to be published by Columbia University Press, Chap. II.

;cond Stage: The Preparation of the Detailed Five-'lan

economic plans for the Soviet Union consist of at least parts: output plans, a financial plan, a capital budget, et, and plans for individual regions. We shall follow preparation, adoption, and execution of only output plans. Later, the others will be touched upon briefly.

Planning is a detailed process, and unless one understands the process, he does not really understand planning. The following discussion of output goal determination, while dealing with the details of planning, is conducted on a fairly general level.

A] How Output Goals Are Set for Individual Products. The determination of output goals is described by Soviet planners as "balance sheet planning";[11] essentially it consists of a determination of output goals in progressively detailed stages. Planners start by estimating the available supply of labor and of many basic materials. These are divided among consumers' goods industries, capital goods industries, and military industries. Thereupon, resources allocated to each of these broad groups are subdivided among more specific industries. For example, labor allocated to consumers' goods industries is allocated to such industry groupings as food fabrication, clothing manufacture, drug production, and the like. Similarly, labor allocated to capital goods industries is subdivided among individual capital goods industries. (In the case of certain key items such as, perhaps, agricultural tractors, the top planners set the output goal directly.) In turn, resources are divided among industries more narrowly defined. For example, planners responsible for the clothing industries might be asked to assign 5 million workers. They will allocate these 5 million workers to produce special clothing for the coldest regions in the country, children's and infants' wear, women's clothing, and men's clothing. These workers would then be divided among more detailed product groupings—such as children's shoes, diapers, men's hats, shirts, and so on.

In this way, a balance of the major factors of production is maintained in their estimated supplies and the quantities allocated to all uses. The allocations are made in stages, first to very broad commodity groupings, and then to narrower subdivisions of those industries.

---

[11] See Kursky, *op. cit.*, p. 126.

The foregoing description reveals the essence of the Soviet planning procedure. With this general picture in mind, it is now possible to explain how planners decide what quantity of specific goods to produce.

(1) Factors that planners take into account in setting output goals for consumers' goods. Planners may aim primarily for maximum military power, or for industrialization at the speediest possible rate. They nevertheless must determine the output of individual consumers' goods. In this sphere, they presumably aim for the greatest amount of satisfaction for the population with a minimum of hardship in production. To achieve this objective, it would be necessary for them to take into account the desires of consumers and the occupational preferences of workers.

(*a*) Consumers' preferences. Rationing has been abolished and consumers in the Soviet Union are free to buy whatever they wish *from the goods available*. The chief point in doubt is how much their wishes determine what goods are made available.

Planners claim to respect consumers' preferences as far as possible in using resources allocated to consumers' goods production. They discover what products will give consumers greatest satisfaction by a wide variety of devices, most of which are similar to market surveys in capitalistic countries.[12] The sincerity of the planners' desires to produce the things consumers want has been questioned; we lack information indicating how strenuous are their efforts to find out what consumers desire. It is difficult to understand why planners would ignore the preferences of consumers, except in cases where consumers' desires conflict with the basic objectives underlying the plan.

As indicated, advertising is employed in the Soviet Union. Apparently one major function of advertising is to encourage people to buy goods whose consumption the planners have special reasons for expanding. For example, industries producing civilian products whose productive facilities would be readily adaptable to military uses might be expanded through extensive advertising of their civilian products. Possibly, advertising is also used to help clear the market of goods whose output was set higher than could easily be sold at the prices initially set. The planners also advertise to speed the acceptance of new products and to overcome the hesitation to try

[12] For a listing of these devices, see E. M. Chossudowsky, "Derationing in the U.S.S.R.," *Review of Economic Studies,* November, 1941, p. 22.

new things. Advertising in the Soviet Union still remains on a very small scale compared to that in the United States.

(*b*) Sacrifices in production. Together with consumers' preferences, planners presumably take relative production costs into account when they set output goals. Costs of production are extremely difficult to define, except in money terms. They are even more difficult to measure. In a fundamental sense, costs consist of activities and experiences that are distasteful or painful, and of the use of materials that could be put to another use. Labor represents by far the largest production cost in all economic systems. The consumption of scarce natural resources is another. How do the Soviet planners measure the costs involved in producing each product? To answer that question, we must know how the irksomeness and scarcity of labor in individual occupations is measured, and then learn how planners attach values to other scarce things used in production, such as natural resources, land, machinery, and loans.

Labor costs depend primarily upon wage rates. These, in turn, vary according to the availability of labor to fulfill output goals. Great shifts have occurred in relative wage rates in the Soviet Union in quite short periods.[13] The magnitude of these changes and the occasions upon which they were made suggest that wage rates do reflect such basic conditions as the relative attractiveness of alternative employments, the location of the labor force in relation to the location of industry, the reluctance of workers to move to distant communities, the skills required in alternative occupations, and the real costs of acquiring these skills. Sometimes real labor costs are reflected in fringe benefits rather than in wage rates.[14]

---

[13] "By 1937, the coal industry, which took thirteenth place among industries in the scale of relative wages in 1928, had risen to second place; heavy engineering had moved from ninth to fifth, and oil, which had previously been eighth, in 1937 was at the head of the list."—Maurice Dobb, *Soviet Planning and Labor in Peace and War* (New York: International Publishers Co., Inc., 1943), pp. 93–94. An order dated August 25, 1950, granted a 20% increase to those employed in coal, oil, iron and steel, building, and other crucial heavy sectors of the economy in the Urals, Siberia, and the Far East. See G. R. Barker, *Soviet Labour,* Bulletins on Soviet Economic Development. No. 6, University of Birmingham, June, 1951, p. 21.

[14] For example, "The government (Soviet) announced today new social security benefits for geological workers, including pay for time lost due to sickness, pensions, bonuses and seniority allowances. The benefits, designed to make the work more attractive and draw new recruits to the geological field, are similar to the benefits that the government ordered for miners in a decree promulgated in September."—*New York Times,* November 18, 1947.

It thus appears that labor costs—and even wage rates themselves—are relatively good indicators of the amount of sacrifice made by workers in production. Wage rates in the Soviet Union apparently could match wage rates in other countries as an indication of the "real costs" of labor.

The method by which the Soviet authorities determine the cost of nonlabor factors of production when they are setting output goals is not clear. Costs assigned to machinery, raw materials, transportation, fuel, and the like seem to be based largely, but not entirely, on labor costs and to a small extent on interest costs.

Equipment costs enter production costs of a product as depreciation charges based upon the cost, mostly for labor, of the equipment. The cost of such things as steel presumably is figured at its total labor, equipment, interest, and transportation cost.

The general principles of Soviet cost calculation do not differ significantly from those used in the United States.[15] The major points of difference between them are these: No money cost is assigned to the depletion of natural resource deposits (the labor costs of removing resources from the ground are, of course, included). Land outside of agriculture seems to bear no direct money cost. Moreover, interest is charged only for working capital for seasonal and other special needs; therefore, most investment in productive enterprises bears no interest charges.

Planners have at their disposal the cost data of individual enterprises. Their decisions about output presumably are influenced by this information.

Although such real sacrifices in production as natural resources, capital funds, and land costs do not enter into money costs, the planners are aware of this fact. Possibly they do take them into account in setting output goals. However, it is important to know in just what way, if at all, such considerations influence output goals. It is extremely difficult to translate qualitative considerations into concrete quantities.

One must not overlook the fact that Soviet planners are influenced by a large body of Marxist economic doctrine. When they take factors into account in a general way, it is likely that they do so differently than would government officials in capitalist countries. Although there have been notable departures from Marxist doctrine

[15] L. E. Hubbard, *Soviet Money and Finance* (London: Macmillan & Co., Ltd., 1936), p. 137.

in the Soviet Union, the views of Soviet economists clearly rest on concepts different from those that underlie the thinking of economists in other countries. They may accordingly have different notions from ours about what factors are relevant and important. One of the writer's major doubts about the quality of Soviet planning stems from his belief that planners are influenced by a desire to conform to Marxist orthodoxy and sometimes unknowingly sacrifice economic efficiency to do so. For example, the Soviet Union does not count distributive activities in calculations of national income. The view that distribution is unproductive is likely to result in insufficient resources being devoted to it. Similarly, Marxian opposition to land rents and increments to the value of land is likely to result in insufficient regard for real sacrifices involved in devoting scarce types of land to particular uses. More important, it seems that until 1949 Soviet planners failed to make much use of cost and price calculations simply because of a doctrinaire objection to bourgeois economics.

(2) Factors influencing output goals for capital goods. Thus far we have dealt with the determination of output goals for consumers' goods. How is the output of individual producers' goods set? We have indicated that broad directives determine what proportion of total resources is to be devoted to capital goods; the particular forms the resources are to take must be determined by planners and set forth in the detailed plan.

Capital investment during any period is governed by the capital budget, which lists specific capital projects. Major investment projects must be approved by the Council of Ministers; others are determined by the planning authorities. Projects requiring approval of high government authorities usually are not purely economic in nature; typically they are of major military or political significance, though sometimes they are huge projects for land reclamation, the construction of large canals, and the like.

Most capital projects are intended to reduce the costs of production. Many enterprises desire new facilities with which to lower production costs. Planners must select from a large number of alternative capital projects. How is their selection made?

Soviet planners require individual ministries to defend their requests for new capital facilities. Among other supporting data, the ministry must estimate the number of years in which a project "would pay for itself." For example, a plant might ask for 100,000 rubles' worth of equipment which would yield savings of 20,000 rubles annually. This project would be described as having a "coefficient of relative effectiveness" of 20 per cent. Projects with the highest coefficients of relative effectiveness—meaning that they will pay for themselves in the shortest time—are given preference.[16] In effect, planners go down the list and approve those projects which will pay off quickest; the exact number of projects undertaken depends upon the total amount of resources to be devoted to cost-reducing investment.

Some capital projects, typically the ones calling for the production of new products, are not intended to reduce production costs. It is impossible to measure the benefits of such projects in terms of the time they take to pay for themselves. Some appraisal must be made of the "value" or "importance" of the new product to the nation. The planners compare the merits of competing claims and make their selection on the basis of considerations that are necessarily highly subjective. (Of course, decisions about investment in new products is subjective even when made by private businessmen in unplanned economies. They cannot have much information to go on, for planners can gather only the same kind of information that businessmen might gather in market surveys.)

In deciding what capital goods to produce, planners apparently use money cost as an indication of the costs involved. In addition, they presumably are influenced by information about the amount of scarce factors of production involved in competing projects. That is, if they know that copper is critically short, they will favor projects not requiring copper, even though on a strictly monetary basis the copper-using project would have been preferable.

3. *The Adoption of a Five-Year Plan*

The manner in which a five-year plan is adopted and made the supreme economic law of the land is relatively simple. First, as indicated, the Soviet Planning Committee[17] submits the plan to representatives of labor, management, and the Communist Party for criticisms and suggestions. Second, the planning agencies review the comments received and revise the plan if, and in whatever ways, they desire. Finally, the plan is submitted to the Politburo (the highest or-

[16] See Schwartz, *op. cit.*, pp. 158–160.

[17] The State Planning Committee (Gosplan) is a subsidiary of the Council of People's Ministers, which is the executive cabinet of the government.

gan of the Communist Party) for final approval and for the resolution of any disputes. Thus, the final plan is reviewed by the government, representatives of workers and management, and the Communist Party.

Literally millions of persons participate in the preparation and adoption of a five-year plan. This process, together with decentralization of the original planning decisions, makes it unnecessary to rely upon the decisions of a single small central group of planners. Information about consumers' desires, production conditions, technological developments, and the like that would ordinarily be unknown to the central planners is made known to them in this way and serious mistakes should be avoided. It is not clear, however, that the planning process allows enough time for full consideration of the many suggestions that are made.

4. *Supervision of the Execution of the Plan*

In the Soviet view "fulfillment supervision" of economic plans is perhaps the most important step in economic planning. According to Molotov, "Unrealistic armchair planning is cheap enough. . . . If the plan is not bound up with plan fulfillment supervision, it becomes a mere scrap of paper. This applies to all our economic organizations and to our entire economic work. By seriously improving our plan fulfillment supervision we shall improve at the same time our economic work and the drawing up of our plans." [18] The Russians apparently rely heavily upon trial and error to arrive at the best results attainable and, therefore, make strenuous efforts to uncover errors and to correct them once they have been found.

Supervision of a plan's fulfillment is entrusted to several agencies. The planning bodies themselves at all levels—with their representatives at all large plants throughout the nation—probably are the best equipped to supervise the plan's execution. In addition, the banks (both the State Bank, which extends short-term credits, and the Industrial Bank, which extends long-term credit) report deviations from plan. The State Bank holds all deposits, and all payments among firms are required to be made on delivery by check. Thus, every delivery of goods is reflected in the State Bank's accounts. Imbalances in the accounts of firms are danger signals that require

[18] V. Molotov, *The Third Five-Year Plan for the Development of the National Economy of the U.S.S.R.* (Moscow: 1939), pp. 20–21.

further investigation. The Industrial Bank similarly is in a position to determine whether investment projects are proceeding according to plan.

Criticism volunteered by individuals is another important form of plan fulfillment supervision. Volunteered comments often appear in the press. The Soviet economy relies heavily upon criticism and everyone is actively encouraged to submit carefully considered observations on every aspect of the economy. Departures from plan in any plant, especially those that can be traced to the shortcomings of one individual or department, are likely to excite comment. The major newspapers maintain a special department for the investigation of complaints. Those found valid and important are published.[19] However, one must not assume that published criticism always has the effect of stimulating remedial action. Apparently there are methods by which lax administrators can escape both the acceptance of blame and the need to remedy an objectionable situation pointed out in the press.[20]

Plans undergo constant revision in order to correct original errors and to adapt to unforeseen circumstances. Perfect plans are not expected; accordingly, the need for revision is anticipated and regular procedures are prescribed for making changes in the original plan. The working out of an economic plan in the Soviet Union thus is accomplished by successive approximations.

5. *The Financial and Labor Plans*

As indicated, a *total economic plan* in the Soviet Union includes many parts. Thus far, we have described only that part of a plan that sets output goals for goods and services. There are also a financial plan for the economy and "budgets" for capital and labor. Although these are complicated and important, little space will be accorded to them here. *Each of these plans is subordinate to and closely tied in with output plans.*

A] The Financial Plan. The financial plan fundamentally translates the output goals into financial terms. Its objectives are to

---

[19] Soviet law requires that acknowledgment of a criticism be made within a few days and answered within a relatively short period.

[20] For the translation of a very ironical and witty letter published in *Pravda,* August 4, 1951, see the *Current Digest of the Soviet Press,* September 15, 1951, pp. 25–26. This letter points out that well-documented and published criticism sometimes has no effect, and only optimists bother to make constructive criticism.

facilitate the achievement of output goals and to achieve a balance between prices of current output (supply) and expenditure (demand). The Soviet Union is a money economy and output plans must be translated into financial terms that allow the desired result. The financial plan incorporates the incentive system of the economy as well as the safeguards against "inflation" and "deflation." (These terms are put in quotes, for they mean different things in planned and in unplanned economies.)

The major components of the Soviet financial plan are the government budget, the credit plan, and the cash plan. The first aims to balance government revenues and expenditures, much like any government budget. It differs from the United States budget in that it applies to a far larger proportion of the economy. The credit plan governs the granting of short- and long-term credits by the banks. The cash plan controls the supply of money in circulation, with the aim of keeping it in line with currency needs.

B] The Labor Budget. The labor budget indicates the supply of and requirements for labor. It includes estimates of additions to the labor force and additional total labor needs and a statement about the number of workers with particular skills that are needed to achieve the output goals. Except for the estimate of additions to the labor force, the labor budget is built up from reports by individual plants of their labor needs for meeting their output goals, and the estimated requirements for agriculture and new capital projects.

C] PRESSURES UPON PLANNERS

The types of decision that planners make have been described. Thus far, we have assumed that planners try to do the kind of job the people in the country would like them to do—that is, try to satisfy the public at large to the utmost of their ability, within the general directives set down for them. Let us, however, inquire into the motives and pressures that might prevent the planners from serving the public interest.

First, it has been charged that government officials in all countries tend to avoid responsibility. There would follow a tendency for planners to abide by past decisions made by others, rather than to advocate changes. That might mean, specifically, that planners tend to make blanket percentage changes in output goals for all consumers' goods, rather than to defend a new principle or specific change in the output of a particular product. For example, if a planner were to argue that the output of shoes should be increased by double the percentage increase in the output of all consumers' goods, he would run the danger of being proved mistaken. The consequences of his mistake might be so serious that he would not willingly take this risk. A secure life for the planner is possibly to be found by sticking to past decisions, which, if they prove to be wrong, can be blamed on someone else.

While this argument doubtless is valid in some cases, there are important pressures on planners operating in the opposite direction. If a planner were fairly certain that the output of shoes should be increased by double the percentage increase desired in other consumers' goods, he would be able to attain recognition and possible promotion by supporting that position. Many persons desire advancement and prestige as much as security. To gain them ordinarily requires novel suggestions and departures from familiar routines. One would expect decisions to be influenced both by persons who preach caution and by persons who favor experimentation.

A second pressure upon planners that might influence their decisions about output in undesired ways is the human tendency to take the easy way out. To do a careful job of planning calls for rigorous thought and the collection of a large body of information; moreover, a conscientious planner must wrestle with many considerations that cannot be reduced to measurement. Planners, like other people, probably prefer easy work to hard work. To attempt the most thorough type of analysis possible might require so much effort that the planner would fall far behind his less conscientious colleagues in getting his work done according to schedule. Planners have a work load to carry, and the more time they devote to each task, the less time they will have to do their other work. In short, careful planning is difficult and time-consuming, and most people do not welcome very hard work. Even when planners do work very hard and collect elaborate information, their decisions cannot be demonstrated conclusively to be the best ones. Many imponderables enter each decision. Accordingly, a planner's conscientiousness might not be recognized and his conclusions might not be accepted. His conscientiousness might simply gain him the reputation of being slow and behind in his work most of the time.

Partly offsetting the tendency of an individual to take the easy way out is the impulse in many persons to do their work competently. Whether it results from an "instinct of workmanship" or "pride in one's work," or whether it simply consists of rising to the challenge in the job, "normal" or "average" individuals rarely take the very easiest way out. Moreover, in any planning group, each individual's work generally is scrutinized by others. Although supervisors may be lazy themselves, they probably do not excuse laziness in their subordinates. Subordinates usually expect their superiors to apply high standards of performance to their work and, therefore, exert themselves more than they enjoy doing. Thus, there are internal pressures within a planning agency that will tend to make individual planners collect all data that can be collected and think carefully and honestly about the significance of the information available.

A third factor that might prevent planners from doing the best possible job is the pressure to set goals that will be fairly certain to be realized. If an industry should fall far behind the goal set, the planner's decision might be questioned. (Of course, the managers of the industry would also be held in suspicion.) To the extent that this consideration operates, planners will be tempted to set their goals relatively low. Here, too, there are contrary pressures. There are very strong incentives in the Soviet Union to call for and strive for large gains in output. Industries frequently fail to meet the goals set for them, the planners seeming to operate on the principle that the harder one tries, the more he achieves. (It should not be forgotten that each plan is submitted to workers and management of each plant, and in that sense has been subjected to a review by those responsible for carrying the plan into effect.)

Fourth, lack of personnel trained to make economic plans could result in deficient planning. While inadequacy of planning personnel was a serious problem at one time, apparently it is no longer so acute.

D] THE ROLE OF PRODUCT PRICES IN THE SOVIET UNION

The role of prices in the Soviet economy has changed substantially since the end of World War II. More and more the Soviet Union is becoming a price system. In January, 1949, new pricing policies were adopted that represent a major step in that direction.[21] Since 1950, subsidies have been abolished.[22] The changed role of prices in

---

[21] M. C. Kaser, "Soviet Planning and the Price Mechanism," *Economic Journal*, March, 1950, pp. 81–91.

[22] *Ibid.*, p. 89.

the Soviet Union can be seen most clearly in the far greater frequency of price changes since 1949, which, prior to then, had been fairly infrequent.[23]

Under the new Soviet policy, prices are established ". . . so as to stimulate increased output of deficit or especially necessary products and simultaneously limit their consumption in production." [24] For example, new prices were set in the coal industry in 1949 ". . . to reflect grades and quality . . . that will make sorting work worth while and make the coal industry directly interested in supplying the national economy with those types and grades it most needs." [25] As these statements imply, factory managers sometimes have enough latitude to vary the proportions in which they produce different articles. By adjusting prices, planners can hold out an incentive for managers to produce the desired commodities.

One Soviet economist wrote in December, 1949, that prices have become the "key to all planning in the U.S.S.R." [26] While this statement may be correct, the Soviet economy still falls far short of a thorough price system. Prices still are set by planning authorities, and do not reflect what might be termed "ordinary market forces." Increases in consumers' desires need not create price inducements to expand output, as is generally the case under full price systems; similarly, increases in real costs need not lead to higher prices. *Prices in the Soviet Union are a tool in the hands of planners rather than an independent mechanism guiding the operations of the economy.* Prices perform more and more, but still not all, of the functions that they perform in the United States.

In the Soviet Union, the prices of consumers' goods and producers' goods differ both in function and in the way they are set. Consumers' goods prices are used primarily as a method of clearing the market of goods that planners decided to produce. If consumers do not buy the output of a product at the price originally set by planners, the price is lowered to clear the market; conversely, shortages are averted by raising the price. Planners need not increase the output of an article because consumers would buy more of it than had been produced—at the price originally planned.

---

[23] Schwartz, *op. cit.*, p. 194.

[24] *Ibid.*, p. 195, quoted from a Soviet source.

[25] Kaser, *op. cit.*, p. 90, quoted from a Soviet coal industry journal.

[26] *Ibid.*, p. 83, quoted from P. Sorokin, "Planning in the Soviet Economy," *Bolshevik*, No. 24, December, 1949, p. 12.

Soviet prices of consumers' goods do not vary directly with production costs. Indeed, a large part of the price of almost every consumers' product is accounted for by the "turnover tax." This tax, the equivalent of a retail excise tax, is the major source of government revenue in the Soviet Union. Turnover taxes vary substantially from product to product. On most consumers' goods they are extremely high. The following table presents typical rates of turnover taxes on selected consumers' goods that were in effect before the war. It shows, for example, that 67 to 71 cents of every dollar paid by a consumer at retail for beef represented the turnover tax. On some products the tax was even higher.[27]

TABLE 3-1

Turnover Tax Rates

Commodity	Per cent	Price basis	Date effective or ordered
Beef	67 –71	retail	Jan. 24, 1940
Butter	60 –66	retail	Apr. 10, 1940
Sugar	73	retail	Jan. 24, 1940
Salt, bulk	70 –80	wholesale	May 1, 1940
Cigarettes	75 –88	wholesale	Jan. 1, 1938
Vodka	84	retail	Jan. 1, 1940
Cotton goods:			
Calico	55	wholesale	June 1, 1937
Others	62 –65	wholesale	June 1, 1937
Shoes from waxed chrome leather	26 –40	retail	July 11, 1940
Soap from untaxed fat:			
Laundry	61 –71	wholesale	Mar. 1, 1936
Toilet	67.5–69.5	wholesale	Mar. 1, 1936

SOURCE: N. Jasny, "The Soviet Price System," *American Economic Review,* December, 1950, p. 853.

[27] Turnover taxes are not simply the difference between production costs and the price that will "clear the market." Another element in this difference is profits—both planned and unplanned. In almost all cases, Soviet planners allow an enterprise to make a profit, which it can use for investment in plant, equipment, and inventories. In addition, some plants, through production economies, incur costs lower than were anticipated. Unplanned profits are shared by management, which gets a share as bonus, and employees, who get a share as welfare services; part is reinvested in the enterprise, and the balance is paid over to the state.

Whereas the prices of consumers' goods are set in a manner that will clear the market, the prices of producers' goods are apparently set at cost.[28] Turnover taxes are not levied on industrial equipment, raw materials, or semifabricated goods; moreover, since 1950, subsidies have not been granted in the Soviet Union. The prices of producers' goods, then, are fairly accurate indications of cost to the economy. They are intended to be, in order that plant managers may select methods of production that involve minimum sacrifice to the community.

Put differently, the prices of producers' goods in the Soviet Union serve two functions. First, they indicate relative cost and thereby guide those making decisions about the methods of production to be employed. Second, the sales of producers' goods indicate the relative needs for various items and thereby guide planners in setting output goals for those products.

In summary, then, prices in the Soviet Union perform three major tasks: they clear the market for consumers' goods, thereby eliminating excessive inventories and avoiding shortages; they indicate the most efficient methods of production to plant managers; and they guide planners in setting output goals. Prices are not, however, permitted to exercise these functions "automatically." Planners directly determine what prices shall be.

E] EFFICIENCY OF PLANNING IN THE SOVIET UNION

Detailed economic planning is very complicated and time-consuming. Consequently, it is exposed to considerable error. Even though it is possible to imagine detailed planning that is precise and internally consistent, highly accurate planning has yet to be achieved in practice. In the Soviet Union, flaws in planning have appeared that cannot be considered trivial. The nature and number of these flaws will now be explored briefly.

First, and perhaps this is the most basic flaw, the Soviet Union has not succeeded in achieving its goals with exactness. Especially during the first two five-year plans, some industries fell far short of fulfillment while others ran substantially ahead. From the standpoint of the effectiveness of planning, overfulfillment of goals shows a failure of the planners to set out to do all they could do. Even in the

[28] The price set on these goods does not equal the cost actually incurred, but the planned cost, which represents the planners' best estimate at the time the plan was drawn up.—Kaser, *op. cit.*, pp. 84–86.

five-year plan that was to have been completed in 1951, but was declared completed in 1950, major deviations from output goals occurred. Outside the field of agriculture, where climatic conditions can be expected to result in deviations from plan, the major underfulfillments of plan took place in the cotton-textile, leather, shoe, hosiery, and automotive industries. Excesses of output over the goals were largest in equipment for iron and steel mills, electric power, copper, and butter production. Table 3-2 shows the discrepancies in major items between the planned output for 1950 and the actual output.

Important parts of the economic program departed very substan-

TABLE 3-2

Deviations between Actual and Planned Output, 1950

Product	Unit of measure	1950 actual output	1950 goal output
I. Shortfalls			
Haulage of timber	million cubic meters	162	190
Paper	thousand tons	1,194	1,340
Cotton fabrics	million meters	3,815	4,686
Silk fabrics	million meters	125	141
Leather shoes	million pairs	205	240
Hosiery*	million pairs	430	580
Motor vehicles*	thousands	405	500
II. Output over goal			
Electric power	billion kilowatt-hours	90	82
Copper	thousand tons	255	225
Equipment for iron and steel mills	thousand tons	134	103
Woolen fabrics	million meters	167	159.4
Butter	thousand tons	325	275
Sugar	million tons	2,515	2,400
Window glass	thousand tons	84.3	80.0
Coal and lignite	million tons	260	250

* H. Schwartz, *Russia's Soviet Economy* (New York: Prentice-Hall, Inc., 1950), p. 567.

SOURCE: Except where otherwise noted, *Economic Survey of Europe in 1950*, United Nations, Department of Economic Affairs, Economic Commission for Europe (Geneva: 1951), p. 39.

tially from the plan even as late as 1950. The wage fund in 1950 was approximately 35 per cent above the level planned. Whereas the plan set the average annual wage at 6,000 rubles, it was over 9,000.[29]

It is therefore not surprising that one noted Soviet economist in late 1940 wrote: "We still have no current economic plan and the necessary guarantee of its fulfillment." He added: "Our planning work to this time is still to a great extent bureaucratic-statistical, separated from economic practice, and it lacks concrete knowledge of the actual situation in the different branches of the economy." [30] Professor Bergson suggests that ". . . to a significant extent the Soviet economy leads a life of its own, quite apart from the will of the planners." [31]

Soviet economists have also criticized regional planning very sharply. One wrote: ". . . until this time (1940) there has been no careful analysis of the distribution of each branch of industry, no analysis of inter-regional connections. Therefore there is also no clearly worked out material regarding the distribution of the different branches of the national economy and regarding the perspective complex development of the economic regions of the country." [32] Recently, presumably around 1949, one Soviet economist wrote: "Inadequate treatment of this interesting theoretic problem (of how to make investment decisions) . . . had had undesirable consequences." [33] In the face of such comments by Soviet planners, it is impossible to conclude that economic planning has been perfected in the Soviet Union.

Comments in the Soviet press carry a variety of complaints which point out other types of planning defects. The following criticisms have been most common in recent years:[34]

1. Output is defective in various ways; apart from complaints about generally low quality (which is not necessarily the fault of the

---

[29] Barker, *op. cit.*, p. 21.

[30] Schwartz, *op. cit.*, p. 140, quoted from Soviet source.

[31] Abram Bergson, "Comments on Gottfried Haberler, 'Business Cycles under Planning'," Universities-National Bureau Conference on Business Cycle Research, November 25–27, 1949.

[32] Schwartz, *op. cit.*, p. 155, from a Soviet source.

[33] Reference by A. Bergson in a book review. See *Economic Journal,* March, 1950, p. 123.

[34] Based primarily on statements in the *Current Digest of the Soviet Press* (see especially September 1, 1951, issue for article by Kosyachenko).

planners), there are charges, for instance, that all clothing of a given size is sometimes made in the same color or style so that any single consumer has no effective choice.

2. Goods produced are distributed faultily so that some areas experience a great glut while others suffer a shortage.

3. Replacement parts for durable goods are often unavailable and inaccessible.

4. Production is interrupted for lack of needed raw materials.

5. Machines are left idle, though they are of a valuable and scarce type.

6. Labor is not fully utilized, because of "padding" of labor requirements and hoarding of labor.

Numerous criticisms of this type reported in the Soviet press indicate that planning errors do occur. However, they do not give a reliable indication of their quantitative importance. The examples cited may be isolated cases; on the other hand, they may be representative of all economic activity.

One would expect gross planning errors to be caught even before a plan goes into effect, because it is possible to "test" plans on paper. If the components of a plan are out of balance, by summing the components on paper one would discover the errors. Formal planning errors, therefore, should be relatively small and not very numerous. On the other hand, there are no reliable tests that can be employed either before, during, or after the planning period to determine whether individual products are produced in the proportions that give the greatest net satisfaction to the population. We can only conjecture about the frequency of this most important type of possible planning error.

IV. DISTRIBUTION OF PERSONAL INCOME IN THE SOVIET UNION

A] DEGREE OF INCOME INEQUALITY

No data are available that describe fully and accurately the size of all personal incomes in the Soviet Union for any current year. We know the incomes received by industrial workers for one month during 1934, and we have scraps of information about incomes of various groups during recent years. However, no full picture of incomes in the Soviet Union can be assembled. Most of the information available describes the incomes of industrial workers; relatively little is known about the incomes of collective farm families.

We know that personal income is distributed quite unequally in the Soviet Union. The Russians admit to and even extol the benefits of substantial income differences.[35] At the top of the income pyramid are artists and scientists and workers who have introduced new production methods (Stakhanovites). The recipients of the lowest incomes are young and unskilled workers.

1. *Incomes of Industrial Workers*

The incomes of industrial wage earners and salaried workers in the Soviet Union in October, 1934, are listed in Table 3-3. At

TABLE 3-3

Distribution of Income among Industrial Workers, 1934

Monthly earnings (in rubles)	Wage earners and salaried workers
Less than 60.1	4.7 %
60.1 to 120	28.4
120.1 to 180	30.5
180.1 to 240	15.8
240.1 to 380	14.6
380.1 to 580	4.7
580.1 to 780	0.9
780.1 to 1,001	0.3
Over 1,100.1	0.08

SOURCE: Adapted from A. Bergson, *The Structure of Soviet Wages* (Cambridge, Mass.: Harvard University Press, 1934), p. 228.

that time, the inequality of workers' incomes was similar in the Soviet Union and in the United States.[36] High inequality of industrial workers' incomes apparently still exists. In 1948, the monthly aver-

[35] J. Stalin, *Problems of Leninism* (New York: International Publishers Co., Inc., 1934), pp. 371–372.

[36] A. Bergson, *The Structure of Soviet Wages* (Cambridge, Mass.: Harvard University Press, 1934).

age earnings of all Soviet workers and employees were about 620 rubles. Reports in the press that year told of outstanding miners receiving monthly incomes of 5,000 to 10,000 or more rubles; top industrial officials probably receive higher incomes.[37]

2. *Incomes of Persons Working for Cooperatives*

Almost everyone not directly employed by the state is engaged in a cooperative enterprise. Most Russians work for cooperatives, industrial as well as agricultural; almost half the population is employed on collective farms. The incomes of persons working in cooperatives depend partly upon the variable revenue obtained by the cooperative. Differences in the productive efficiency of individual cooperatives result in a different level of average income for members of the cooperative. Each individual's income is determined primarily by a piece-rate system. The incomes of collective farmers depend, in addition, upon the value of the produce they raise upon their private plots of land. Not all collective farmers are equally efficient in tending their own private plots or equally astute in selling their output.

3. *Incomes of Professionals and Artists*

College teachers are reported to receive between 4,000 and 5,000 rubles monthly (about six to eight times as much as the average industrial worker). Accountants are employees of the state and their incomes are similar to those of other professional planners. They do not reach the great heights of the most successful certified public accountants in this country. Doctors in the Soviet Union are government employees. They can, however, engage in private practice. While their pay is high in comparison with the average Russian's income, they do not approach the extremely high levels attained by the most successful doctors in capitalist countries.

Authors of successful literary works probably receive higher incomes than college teachers and other professionals.[38] Artists and scientists are the most highly rewarded of all Soviet citizens. In addition to relatively high monetary incomes, they receive honors which also carry economic benefits such as automobiles, vacations, special housing, and the like.

---

[37] Schwartz, *op. cit.*, pp. 466–467.
[38] *Ibid.*

B] DETERMINANTS OF PERSONAL INCOME IN THE SOVIET UNION

Personal incomes in the Soviet Union apparently are determined by four major factors: scarcity, productivity, personal and political influence, and public services received. Each of these factors will be discussed in turn and will be followed by a discussion of tax rates, income from property, and the role of bargaining power.

1. *Influence of Scarcity on Personal Incomes*

"Wages are changed as seems necessary to effectuate government policy and achieve particular production ends, rather than in response to direct pressure from worker." [39] Workers who possess a rare skill or are employed in a region where their skills are scarce receive relatively high incomes.

2. *Influence of Productivity on Personal Incomes*

About 75 per cent of all workers in the Soviet Union are paid on a piece-rate basis, thus making for a very close connection between income and productivity. The Russians often vary their piece rates so that the more a worker produces beyond his daily "norm," the higher the piece rate. This system is described as a progressive piece-rate system, and it magnifies the influence of productivity upon income differences. Workers doing the same job in the Soviet Union, therefore, may earn widely different incomes.

3. *Personal and Political Influence*

Communist writings are highly critical of personal and political influence in capitalist societies. The Soviet Union, however, has not succeeded in preventing these factors from arising to interfere with a pure "merit system." Articles and letters in the Soviet press charge or imply that high posts sometimes go to personal favorites rather than to the most worthy persons. Moreover, members of the Communist Party seem to be strongly favored over nonmembers for important posts. It is difficult to assess the extent to which personal and political influence affects the distribution of personal income because of the lack of evidence.

---

[39] *Ibid.*, p. 458.

4. *Eligibility for Free Public Services*

A substantial share of a Soviet citizen's income takes the form of vital services provided free by the state, or services that are made available far below cost. It is reported that " . . . state expenditures for sick benefits, maternity leave, free education and free medical service actually add more than one-third of their wages to the income of the working people." [40] In addition to these items must be included paid vacations, maintenance of children's institutions (nurseries and kindergartens), grants to families having many children, and expenditures for cultural and other services made from factory directors' funds. Housing apparently is subsidized, for Soviet citizens pay no more than 2 to 3 per cent of their income for housing,[41] which, however, is ordinarily small in space and low in quality. State social insurance is provided for all Soviet workers and employees without special fees or taxes; these are paid by the enterprise or institution at the expense of the state.[42]

5. *Personal Income Tax Rates in the Soviet Union*

The Soviet Union employs a personal income tax. Compared with rates in the United States and the United Kingdom, the Russian income tax is low and not very progressive. It appears that the government does not want to weaken the incentive effects of its compensation system by highly progressive taxation. The latest personal income tax rates are presented in Table 3–4.

Members of industrial cooperatives pay rates 10 per cent higher than those listed in the table. Writers, artists, and the like pay the same rates as hired workers, but for them the progression of rates continues beyond monthly incomes of 1,000 rubles.[43]

Taxes on income received by collective farmers from their own private subsidiary sources—personal plots, livestock, and nonagricultural earnings—are very progressive. On August 30, 1951, these rates were increased. Rates vary from 12 per cent on the lowest incomes to marginal rates of 48 per cent.[44]

---

[40] Statement by V. V. Kuznetsov, chairman of the All-Union Central Council of Trade-Unions, reported in the *U.S.S.R. Information Bulletin,* February 10, 1950, p. 80.

[41] *Ibid.,* p. 81. This figure is lower than the figure generally cited of 4 to 5 per cent.

[42] *Ibid.,* p. 78.

[43] Schwartz, *op. cit.,* p. 419.

[44] *Current Digest of the Soviet Press,* October 6, 1951, pp. 6–8.

TABLE 3-4

Income Tax Rates for Hired Workers

Monthly wage in rubles	Monthly tax
150– 200	2.5 rubles plus 5.5% of excess over 150
201– 300	5 " " 6% " " " 200
301– 400	11 " " 7% " " " 300
401– 500	18 " " 8% " " " 400
501– 700	26 " " 10% " " " 500
701–1,000	46 " " 12% " " " 700
1,001 and higher	82 " " 13% " " " 1,000

SOURCE: H. Schwartz, *Russia's Soviet Economy* (New York: Prentice-Hall, Inc., 1950), p. 419. The date to which these rates apply is not indicated; they probably were in effect up to the outbreak of World War II.

6. *Property Incomes in the Soviet Union*

Although Marxists in capitalist countries deplore property income, it is possible to receive income from the ownership of property in the Soviet Union. Holders of most government bonds receive 2 per cent interest. Bonds issued in 1950 allowed holders to participate in annual lotteries; over their twenty-year term, 35 per cent of all bonds will win prizes and be redeemed by the state. The remaining will be redeemed at face value without interest. The maximum income that a Soviet citizen may receive in the form of interest on government bonds is likely to be moderate,[45] though apparently it is not limited by law.

Moreover, interest is paid on savings deposits in the Soviet Union. If deposited for specified terms of not less than six months, they earn 5 per cent interest.[46]

7. *Influence of Market Power on Personal Incomes in the Soviet Union*

Market power has little influence on workers' incomes in the Soviet Union. Labor unions do not influence the total amount paid to workers. Total wage payments for each enterprise are set in the general plan. Unions do, however, strongly influence the manner in

[45] Dobb, *op. cit.*, p. 9.

[46] Loucks and Hoot, *op. cit.*, p. 526.

which these payments are made according to individual skills of workers.[47] It seems that wage rates, or piece rates, are varied in ways that will assist in achieving the output goals.

At the present time, the primary activities of Soviet labor unions consist in encouraging increases in productivity, participating in formulation of plans, providing social and cultural facilities for workers, and training workers. Soviet economists argue that labor unions serve a different function in capitalist and socialist economies. In a socialist state, when they win wage increases, they do not take away the profits of owners, but they take income from other workers. On the other hand, those who argue that unions have been rendered impotent in the Soviet Union claim that Soviet citizens have become helpless against whatever decisions are made by government bureaucrats, who now have the power to push wages as low as they wish.

Income inequality in the Soviet Union, while quite considerable, is far less than in the United States. Inequality of worker income is possibly greater in the Soviet Union, but incomes from property are nominal. In the United States, the highest incomes come almost entirely from property. In the Soviet Union no person receives the equivalent of, say, a million dollars of income a year.

It is difficult to judge whether income inequality in the Soviet Union is as low as it could be made without injury to work incentives. Planners apparently try to reduce income inequality by substituting honors for money payments and by offering inducements in the form of preferential housing privileges, especially long vacations, and the like. The very high rewards to Soviet scientists and artists, people peculiarly unresponsive to monetary incentives the world over, suggest that Soviet planners are not determined to push income inequality to an absolute minimum. Put differently, they seem, at this stage at least, to be far more concerned with maximum total output than with equality of income distribution.

[47] Professor Schwartz takes a different view. He states: "All direct influence of unions on wages is thus eliminated."—*Op. cit.*, p. 457.

V. PRODUCTIVE EFFICIENCY IN THE SOVIET UNION

Responsibility for productive efficiency in Soviet enterprises is lodged with the plant manager. Not only does he have the duty to make production efficient; he is given considerable incentive to do so. Central planners also indirectly influence productive efficiency, for they allocate the money for production costs.

In selecting methods of production, plant managers are directed to keep money costs to a minimum.[48] Thus, the internal operations of each firm are guided by price considerations. In an effort to use money costs as a reliable indicator of production efficiency, the Soviet planners lay important stress on developing the science of cost accounting.

The compensation of most Soviet factory managers is linked to their ability to reduce production costs below those set for their enterprise in the general plan. Managers obtain financial bonuses based upon the unplanned profits earned by their enterprise. "In certain cases these bonuses (to directors, managers and foremen) run as high as 200 per cent of the monthly salaries." [49]

Managers are urged to stimulate worker "competition" in an effort to raise output. Since most workers are paid by a piecework system that frequently is progressive, a strong financial incentive to increase efficiency is provided to workers. In addition, a large proportion of the unplanned profits obtained by an enterprise goes into the "director's fund," which is used to expand industrial facilities and to provide cultural, social, and welfare services for workers. (The remainder is returned to the state, after bonuses to workers and executives have been paid.)

The efficiency of each Soviet plant reflects the zeal and intelligence of the plant manager, the quality of the industrial equipment, and the industriousness of the labor force. Apparently wide differences in productive efficiency exist. In the third quarter of 1949, it cost 70 per cent more to produce pig iron in Ukrainian metallurgical plants than at Magnitogorsk. The cost of a ton of petroleum from Baku in 1941 was 16.6 rubles, whereas a ton produced from the Syzran oil field cost 39.7 rubles. Data for 1940 indicate that coal pro-

[48] Schwartz, *op. cit.*, p. 191.

[49] Earl R. Sikes, *Contemporary Economic Systems* (New York: Henry Holt & Company, Inc., 2d ed., 1951), p. 416.

duced in the eastern regions of the Soviet Union cost 58 to 71 per cent less than the average for the entire country.[50] While these examples are drawn from industries where the quality of natural resources rather than the degree of productive efficiency might account for the observed difference in cost, they are apparently not out of line with what is found in other industries not heavily dependent upon natural resources.

Information is exchanged freely among plant managers in the Soviet Union, and the results of technical research are made available to all of them who are interested. Moreover, improvements in plant design and layout and general productive arrangements are, as a conscious policy, disseminated from plant to plant.

To insure centralized responsibility for productive efficiency, both the power and the responsibility of the plant director have been progressively increased. ". . . he has extensive powers of disciplining, transferring, and dismissing workers in accordance with labor laws and rules laid down by the higher governmental bodies. He appoints and dismisses his department heads and other assistants."[51]

Productive efficiency is high even by American standards in the best-run Soviet plants,[52] but in many it falls far below American standards. No over-all assessment can be made with confidence. While numerous instances of inefficient operation are mentioned in the Soviet press, we do not know how many plants in this and other countries are equally inefficient. The major types of productive inefficiencies that admittedly exist in the Soviet Union help to illuminate its economic system. They are listed below.[53]

1. Labor turnover, absenteeism, and tardiness have been grossly excessive in many plants.

2. Administrative inefficiency is not uncommon and takes the following forms:

a. Work is poorly organized.

---

[50] Schwartz, *op. cit.*, p. 191.

[51] Loucks and Hoot, *op. cit.*, p. 498.

[52] Gen. Walter Bedell Smith, *My Three Years in Moscow* (Philadelphia: J. B. Lippincott Company, 1943). General Smith wrote that his favorable impression of Soviet productive efficiency in some plants was confirmed by Eric Johnston and by American engineers and industrialists who visited Soviet plants. See pp. 141–142. Wendell Willkie reached a similar verdict. See *One World* (New York: Simon & Schuster, Inc., 1943), p. 61.

[53] Based upon the *Current Digest of the Soviet Press*. See also Loucks and Hoot, *op. cit.*, pp. 606–609; and Smith, *op. cit.*, p. 140.

b. There are long delays in repair of needed equipment.

c. Unneeded labor is hoarded.

d. There is failure to master the mass production of new machines and a violation of blueprints.

e. "Flow of production" methods are not widely adopted.

f. New high-capacity equipment frequently remains idle.

g. "Storming"—that is, meeting production goals by extreme speed during the last days of the month—is widespread.

h. Superfluous stocks of raw materials and finished goods are accumulated in manufacturing plants.

i. Plants are not kept clean and products consequently spoil.

j. There is failure to analyze correctly the qualities of raw materials before setting up plants to process them.

k. Maintenance of equipment is neglected to achieve dramatic production records.

l. Undue emphasis is put upon quantity of output at the expense of quality.

m. Skilled workers are employed at unskilled tasks.

n. Administrative branches have swollen staffs.

3. The low quality of manufactured goods has been due only in part to poor design. Most shoddy merchandise has been the result of poor production methods and to overleniency of product inspectors.

4. Underemployment and unemployment do exist. Although planning makes the elimination of unemployment theoretically possible, it does not automatically insure full employment. Some Soviet workers apparently have not been kept fully occupied, even though the economy as a whole has, if anything, suffered from a labor shortage.

To avoid unemployment, planners must set individual output goals that all together require neither fewer nor more workers than desire to work. Clearly, if the output goals call for only 90 per cent of the available workers, one of every ten will be out of work, or workers will do only 90 per cent as much work as they would if planning were perfect. If the goals are set higher than can be achieved, some industries will not receive all the materials required to meet their planned output, and their labor force, which will have been geared to their goals, will not be fully occupied. Only "near-perfect" planning could escape unemployment due to setting output goals either too high or too low.

Unemployment is likely to be hard to detect in the Soviet Union, even by the authorities. Work probably is spread fairly evenly among workers attached to an enterprise, and unemployment takes the form of the population working less than it would have if planning had been perfect.

Thus, a condition analogous to unemployment does exist in the Soviet Union; this condition is a loss of output due to partial idleness of labor. However, the burden of unemployment does not fall on one segment of the population. Moreover, unemployment or underemployment is not cumulative as it is in capitalist countries.[54]

VI. PROGRESSIVENESS OF THE SOVIET ECONOMY

The Soviet planners determine what proportion of the nation's resources to devote to research and to the study of technological methods in other parts of the world. While comparisons of expenditures by different countries are hazardous, it appears that the Soviet Union spent as much for research in 1947 as was spent in the United States in the same year.[55] In view of the much smaller national income of the Soviet Union (it is roughly one fourth our own), the latter nation seems to be making a relatively greater effort to develop and apply new technology than the United States is currently making.

Partly as a result of concentrated research efforts, the Soviet economy has increased its productivity very rapidly. Table 3-5 compares the per capita output of industrial workers in the Soviet Union with that in the United States, Great Britain, and Germany.

Part of the large rise in Soviet industrial productivity must be attributed to its early backwardness. Simply by initiating procedures used in other nations, the Soviet Union could make great progress. It has been "catching up" to other nations, and henceforth its technological advance probably will slow down considerably.

---

[54] Capitalist countries could adopt measures, no more complicated than near-perfect planning in the Soviet Union, that would virtually eliminate business cycles. Measures needed to combat business cycles are less politically feasible in the United States than in the Soviet Union.

[55] Report by the President's Scientific Research Board, *Science and Public Policy*, vol. I, August, 1947, pp. 5–6.

TABLE 3-5

Industrial Productivity of the Soviet Union Compared with that of the United States, Great Britain, and Germany

Year	Soviet productivity as a percentage of productivity in		
	United States	Great Britain	Germany
1928	16.2%	55.3%	44.6%
1932	26.2	70.7	60.5
1937	40.5	103.1	97.0

SOURCE: H. Schwartz, *Russia's Soviet Economy* (New York: Prentice-Hall, Inc., 1950), p. 471; the results came originally from a Soviet source.

Moreover, the Soviet Union's industrial equipment probably is the newest in the world—on the average. It has not been held back, as have some other industrial nations, by an unwillingness to scrap useful but outmoded equipment. As a result, most Soviet industrial plants use modern machinery.

Dramatic evidence of the technological prowess of the Soviet Union is to be found in its military innovations and the quality of its military equipment. The Katushka, a multirocket firing artillery piece, was introduced by the Russians during World War II; they were able to produce the atomic bomb before any country except the United States and much more rapidly than was expected. Moreover ". . . they have a jet engine in the MIG 15 (fighter plane) that is superior to any jet engine that we have today." [56]

"The Germans considered the Soviet tanks the best in the world—even including their own—and our own artillerymen paid tribute to the excellence of the Russian artillery material and technique of fire. French air officers . . . classed the YAK fighter as the best short-range interceptor pursuit plane in use during the war." [57] In addition, the Russians pioneered in the field of air-borne operations and military rockets.

As these results show, industry in the Soviet Union was transformed by the Communist regime from one of the most backward in the world to one of the most advanced. This result is hardly surprising in view of the high importance Marxists attribute to

[56] Statement by Gen. Hoyt S. Vandenberg, Secretary for Air, before the Senate Foreign Relations and Armed Services Committees on May 28, 1951, reported in the *New York Times,* May 29, 1951.

[57] Smith, *op. cit.,* p. 318.

"science." Marxists are, in one respect, the forerunners of the modern technocrats. They believe that if science were harnessed for the welfare of man rather than for his "exploitation," everyone could have a very prosperous life. Indeed, they believe the potentialities of science are so great that total output could be made large enough that everyone could have as much as he wanted. (It seems that the leaders of the Soviet Union are still looking forward to the time when they will reach a stage of "pure communism," under which individuals will produce according to their ability and partake of output according to their needs.)

VII. THE ALLOCATION OF PRODUCTIVE AGENTS AMONG OCCUPATIONS IN THE SOVIET UNION

Even critics of the Soviet regime admit that up to the early 1930's individuals were essentially free to enter any occupation in which they could obtain employment in the Soviet Union. However, some restrictions on occupational choice have been created since 1933.

A] RESTRICTIONS ON OCCUPATIONAL CHOICE IN THE SOVIET UNION

From 1933 on, students graduating from a university or technical school have had to work for five years at a definite point of production fixed by the planning commissariat to which the school was subordinate.[58] In October, 1940, a law was enacted that allowed the authorities to order young men between the ages of fourteen and seventeen to enter trade and railroad schools for two years of training designed to make them skilled workers; the law permitted the authorities to require workers to remain in the occupations for which they were trained for at least four years after completion of training. "So far as possible, the Soviet government attempts to get voluntary recruits for these schools, stressing that all students' expenses are paid during training. The deficit between government labor requirements and the number of volunteers is made up through compulsory draft." [59] It is not clear how this State

---

[58] Baykov, *op. cit.*, p. 352, *nn.*

[59] Schwartz, *op. cit.*, p. 449.

Labor Reserves law has operated; specifically, the extent to which the state is able to obtain volunteers and the degree to which persons are directed into occupations that are unattractive to them have not been reported reliably.

The State Labor Reserves measure just described indicates an essential characteristic of the Soviet Union. It suffers from a shortage of skilled workers in many, if not most, lines. Accordingly, opportunities would seem to exist for qualified persons to become skilled workers in fields in which they are interested. On the other hand, reliance on a draft (to the extent that this exists) suggests that compensation for skilled workers is artificially low in that it is insufficient to attract persons to enter those fields voluntarily.

Other restrictive decrees were enacted in 1940. Workers and technicians could be transferred from one enterprise to another by government ministries; voluntary quitting was forbidden to all workers and employees in state, cooperative, and social enterprises and institutions. Permission to leave one's employment had to be obtained, and the manager could refuse such requests. Despite these laws, Soviet officials still complain of high labor turnover, a fact suggesting that these restrictions are not invoked except in an emergency.[60] On the other hand, it would be surprising if a plant manager who had no surplus labor would release competent workmen simply because they said they didn't like the work or hoped to make more money or get better housing elsewhere.

The Soviet press has carried complaints by workers who were not free to work where they wished. A common complaint is that workers are assigned to jobs without regard to the skills they have acquired. One worker complained that he was shifted to six different jobs in eighteen months. A group of graduate carpenters wrote that they had been taught a good specialty but were deprived of the opportunity to employ it, even though their type of labor was in short supply. It appears from these cases, which may or may not be representative, that the Russians use workers in the State Labor Reserve to do jobs for which labor temporarily is in short supply. Another complaint is that graduates of training schools live in difficult and sometimes intolerable circumstances. One student wrote that the room in

[60] Loucks and Hoot, *op. cit.*, pp. 559–560. Moreover, a delegation of British workers that visited the Soviet Union in 1950 stated categorically: "There is no direction of labor, whatever."—See *Russia with Our Own Eyes* (New York: S. R. T. Publications, 1951), p. 85.

which he was lodged had too little furniture, the bed linen was rarely changed, the workers themselves had to wash their linen, there was no sports equipment, no wash basins, no tanks for boiling water; moreover, the rooms in general were filthy.[61]

B] CONDITIONS FACILITATING FREE OCCUPATIONAL CHOICE

In the Soviet Union it is easy for competent persons to receive further training; they are not dependent upon their own or their parents' financial resources. Academic education and vocational training are freely available to all highly qualified persons. Students entering professional schools obtain scholarships if they can meet entrance requirements; they are also paid a modest income during the period of their training. Similarly, youths can volunteer to enter any of a variety of training programs that will make them skilled workers. They are also paid during their training program. (Entrance into these training programs likewise is contingent upon meeting the admissions requirements.) Students who have not shown promise in their studies must pay a nominal tuition.[62]

The high proportion of students in universities and technical schools who receive scholarships is indicated by the following table.

TABLE 3-6

Percentage of the Total Number of Students in Receipt of Scholarships and Maintenance Grants

Institution	1933	1939
Universities and higher technical schools	50	91
Technical and other secondary schools for the training of cadres (technicians)	60	86

SOURCE: Adapted from A. Baykov, *The Development of the Soviet Economic System* (New York: The Macmillan Company, 1947), p. 347.

The Russians assert that theirs is a merit system and that the

[61] All the foregoing is taken from a *New York Times* story which is based upon an anti-Communist newsletter, *The Baltic Review,* of Stockholm, Sweden. See *New York Times,* June 3, 1951, p. 82.

[62] "During the War, fees were imposed and living cost stipends were granted only to those who needed them and maintained a certain level of marks. The reasons given for this change were the increasing money incomes of the people and the desire to divert students into the trade schools."—Loucks and Hoot, *op. cit.,* p. 602. The postwar situation is not clear.

choice jobs in the economy go to persons who demonstrate the greatest competence. They show that individuals from all walks of life are eligible to, and actually do, attain the highest elective offices and the greatest honors that the nation bestows. They claim that they have largely eliminated nepotism. It would be remarkable if this claim were fully valid. That it probably is not is suggested by a cartoon in a Russian magazine showing a "dandy" sitting on a park bench talking to a companion and explaining that his uncle is arranging a soft berth for him in the ministry where the uncle holds a high post.[63]

The exposure of an official to criticism in the press for playing favorites probably restrains most persons from doing as much to help their relatives as they might like to do. Nepotism is criticized in the Soviet Union, whereas it is taken for granted in the capitalist countries. As a result, there is very probably less of it in the Soviet Union than in the United States.

On balance, therefore, it seems that in the Soviet Union individuals are allocated among occupations primarily on the basis of their personal preferences and talents; however, the government has imposed strict restrictions upon labor movements—especially on those persons whose training was financed by the government. Moreover, the government has enacted legislation that could be used virtually to freeze workers in their present jobs and could compel them to take jobs considered unattractive. On the other hand, severe limitations on occupational choice in capitalist countries in the form of inability to afford necessary training and the appointment of persons to top posts because of personal or political influences seem to be relatively infrequent.

VIII. AN EVALUATION OF THE SOVIET UNION

Now that we have described the manner in which the Soviet economy operates, let us evaluate its over-all performance. Communists took control of the Russian economy in 1917. A sufficiently long period has elapsed since then to reveal the potentialities of the Communist system. Before the evidence describing what has happened under the Communists in Russia can be interpreted, it is necessary to formulate criteria by which the economy is to be judged.

[63] The cartoon is reproduced in the *New York Times* Sunday Magazine Section, April 15, 1951, p. 13.

A] CRITERIA FOR JUDGMENT

First, the Soviet Union can be judged by the avowed goals of those who led the Revolution, or by the ends we hope to achieve by capitalism. We should judge Communism both by whether it has done what it claimed to do and by whether it is the type of economy we would like for ourselves. If the system gives the Russians what they desire, it cannot be considered a failure in the Soviet Union. If, however, it does not give what we would want, it must be adjudged a poor system for the United States, no matter how the Russians view its accomplishments.

Second, we must establish what could legitimately be expected if Communism were successful. It must be recognized that the Russians were the first to attempt detailed and thorough economic planning. They had to blaze a trail in an uncharted field. It was to be expected that progress would be slow at best, for the job they tried to do was enormous and they attempted it under highly adverse circumstances.

How long should the Soviet leaders be willing to spend in devising an efficient planning machine? Should they be adjudged failures if they failed to work out efficient planning procedures within six months? within six years? in sixty years? If the machinery finally devised could solve all but trivial economic problems, it conceivably would justify sixty years of sacrifice. (And then again, individuals might properly decline to sacrifice themselves so that later generations might enjoy a higher standard of living.) It is clearly impossible to determine how long it is worth waiting for an efficient economic system to be worked out. That being the case, it is difficult to evaluate the Soviet economy.

B] A REVIEW OF SOVIET ACCOMPLISHMENTS

The accomplishments of the Soviet Union will be discussed with the government's objectives as a backdrop. First we shall investigate the extent to which the Soviet Union has progressed toward its economic goals; thereafter we shall discuss its noneconomic achievements.

1. *Economic Accomplishments of the Soviet Union*

Soviet leaders, since their advent to power, have set three major economic objectives for themselves: (1) to industrialize rapidly; (2) to develop planning machinery, procedures, and principles;

and (3) to increase output greatly. Progress made toward each of these objectives will be discussed in turn.

A] Degree of Industrialization. Industrialization is best measured by the changing proportion of persons engaged in agriculture and in industry. While a detailed description of the occupational distribution of the Soviet population is lacking, the rapid industrialization of the Soviet Union can be seen in the increased number of workers in nonagricultural undertakings over a short period. The following table shows, for example, that the number of persons engaged in industry more than tripled during the nine years between 1928 and 1937. (Total population increased about 20 per cent during this period.) All the nonagricultural occupations increased substantially more than the total population; the proportion of the labor force engaged in agriculture declined correspondingly.

TABLE 3-7

Occupational Distribution of Soviet Labor Force, 1928–1937

Branch	1928	1937
Industry	3.1%	10.1%
Construction	0.7	2.0
Railways	1.0	1.5
Waterways	0.1	0.18
Other transport	0.2	1.1
Communications	0.1	0.38
Education	0.8	2.3
Health services	0.4	1.1
State, administrative, and other institutions	1.2	2.5
Banking institutions	0.1	0.19

SOURCE: H. Schwartz, *Russia's Soviet Economy* (New York: Prentice-Hall, Inc., 1950), p. 444.

Roughly 85 per cent of all Russians were engaged in agriculture in 1917.[64] After World War II, over half of all Soviet citizens were employed outside agriculture.[65] This shift of labor force un-

[64] Sikes, *op. cit.*, p. 343.

[65] Smith, *op. cit.*, p. 132. Loucks and Hoot, on the other hand, state: "Two thirds of the workers of the Soviet Union are engaged in agricultural production."—*Op. cit.*, p. 480.

questionably represents the most speedy industrialization of a major nation the world has known. It probably was also the most painful conversion experienced by any nation, for it took place when living standards were very low.

B] Development of Planning Machinery, Procedures, and Principles. Another major objective of the Soviet leaders was the creation of a planned economy. Despite many handicaps, to be mentioned presently, the Communists have had the long period since 1917 to experiment with planning procedures, establish planning machinery, and formulate principles and procedures. It seems legitimate to judge the Soviet Union to a large extent by the efficiency of its planning. Unfortunately there is far from general agreement on this point. The Russians unquestionably have demonstrated that planning could work well enough to "keep going"; however, the efficiency of their planning arrangements is in real dispute. As already noted, even the Russians themselves have been critical of them. Foreign observers reach widely different conclusions about the effectiveness of Soviet planning. None, however, claim that the Russians have closely approached great efficiency in planning; some say that the economy is virtually unplanned, while others say that the planners achieve the results they desire with only minor wastes and mistakes. We simply lack sufficient information to evaluate Soviet planning procedure with confidence. The author would describe planning in the Soviet Union in 1952 as rough and clumsy, though probably resting on sound methods and conceptions.

C] Expansion of Industrial Output. In assessing the accomplishments of the Soviet Union, and most especially in evaluating its output record under Communist leadership, the conditions between 1917 and 1951 must be taken into account. The period of Communist rule has been among the most disturbed in all Russian, and perhaps world, history.

The many disturbances during this period influence what achievements we could legitimately expect from the Soviet regime. Between 1917 and 1921, the Russians fought a war against Germany, engaged in a bloody and incredibly destructive civil war, and were invaded by foreign armies. For a large part of its life, the Soviet Union was denied diplomatic recognition by other nations and was able to obtain very little economic assistance from abroad. Moreover, between about 1937 and 1941, the Soviet Union greatly intensified efforts to create a strong military establishment because of an increased likelihood of war. The growth of the armed forces and military supplies after 1937 came primarily at the expense of nonmilitary achievements. Between 1941 and 1945, the Soviet Union suffered enormous damage to life and property during the conflict with Germany. Since V-E Day, the Soviet Union has been engaged in a "cold war" that has made it advisable—from the Soviet point of view—to maintain military forces in great strength and to produce large quantities of military equipment. Thus, during a substantial part of the period since the founding of the Soviet Union, conditions have been extremely difficult by any standard. One must not expect the Soviet Union to have achieved since 1917 what could have been expected if the period had been one of uninterrupted international and domestic tranquillity.

(1) Sources of error in evaluating the Soviet production record. In assessing the performance of the Soviet Union, we must rely almost exclusively upon statistical results reported by the Soviet authorities. We have ample evidence that they believe economic facts to have high military value to potential enemies; they have actually prohibited the publication of many such types of information.[66] *On the other hand, experts on the Soviet economy are almost all in full agreement that Soviet output information is not falsified.* Information is suppressed, and some that is published is misleading, but direct falsification is probably not practiced.[67]

Many of the errors made in assessing the results claimed by the Soviet Union result from studying "synthetic" statistics; synthetic statistics do not describe production of a product directly in terms of concrete units of output; instead, they are "indexes" that combine in a single number the output of many products. The preparation of an index is, at best, a complicated process, and often more than one method of computation is possible. (The major problems faced in the construction of an index are the selection of items to be included and the "weight" to be attached to each one.)

---

[66] The States Secrets Decrees of June, 1947, increased the severity of the already severe penalties for the unauthorized disclosure of the most routine economic information. See Smith, *op. cit.,* p. 133.

[67] Professor Alexander Gerschenkron, one of the leading experts on the Soviet Union, writes: "Serious students of the Russian economy agree that the Russian practice is to withhold certain statistical information rather than to falsify it."—"The Soviet Indices of Industrial Production," *Review of Economics and Statistics,* November, 1947, p. 217.

Another possible source of error is the exclusive reliance on measurements in terms of percentage increases from a preceding period. The Soviet authorities sometimes compare current output with that of years when the output of some products was virtually nil; these comparisons show huge percentage increases, to which it is easy to attach undue significance. On the other hand, in studying the output of products that have been made for a long time, or whose output we know to be large in absolute terms, percentage increases are a satisfactory source of information. Indeed, one's mind typically tries to change absolute numbers into percentage terms in assessing production information.

If we stick to specific products, preferably to those whose output is reported in physical terms, and if, when dealing with products whose output is reported only in terms of percentage changes, we concern ourselves only with those whose output is substantial, we should not go far astray. We must beware of statistical indexes unless we know precisely how they are constructed.[68]

To determine how much output has changed in the Soviet Union, it is probably best to study first *general indicators of output.* These report the production of goods and services that tend to vary with activity in virtually all lines of work. Electric power generated, freight movements, and steel output probably are the best indicators of the rate of industrial activity in *all* lines. Thereupon, we can examine the output of specific lines of business, taking care to distinguish between consumers' goods and capital goods industries. These groups of industries often change by widely different proportions and sometimes move in different directions in the Soviet Union.

(2) General indicators of change in Soviet output. General indicators of output in the Soviet Union show great expansions since the Soviet government took power. Whether one compares current output with output in 1913 or with output immediately after the devastating civil war, he finds that electric power production expanded enormously; specifically it multiplied more than 45 times since 1913 and is 180 times as large as it was in 1921. Steel output in 1950 was 6½ times as great as in 1913 and over 50 times what it was in 1920. (Steel production regained its 1913 level only in 1927–1928.) Railroad freight multiplied 9 times between 1913

[68] Most of the Soviet indexes are recognized by the Russians themselves to include an upward bias. Since the "cold war" is partly a statistical war, it is unlikely that the Russians will recalculate their indexes to show a much smaller rate of progress than they had been claiming heretofore.

and 1950 and 25 times between 1922–1923 and 1950. None of these general indicators was produced in extremely small quantities in 1913, for they are old and basic industries.

The increase in total Soviet output, judged by these three indicators, would vary widely according to the specific indicator selected. It matters a great deal whether more than a forty-five-fold expansion took place between 1913 and 1950, as one would gather from electric power production, or a sixfold increase, as in the case of steel. Any of these indexes, however, supports the conclusion that output has expanded very greatly since the Communist Revolution. This general conclusion is borne out by the information describing changes in the output of other products. The three tables that follow present considerable information about the output of major products in the Soviet Union. Producers' and consumers' goods are shown separately.

TABLE 3-8

Physical Output of Basic Industries in the Soviet Union

Period	Electric power production*	Steel output†	Railroad freight‡
1913	1.9	4.2	65.7
Post–civil war	0.5 (1921)	0.2 (1920)	23.5 (1922–1923)
Mid-1930's	21.0 (1934)	9.7 (1934)	169.3 (1932)
1940	48.3	18.3	415.0
1945	43.2	11.2	314
1952	104.0§	31.0§	585 (1950)
1955 (targets)	168.0	44.2	

* Billion kilowatt-hours. † Million metric tons. ‡ Billion ton kilometers.
§ Malenkov's speech to Nineteenth Congress of Soviets.

SOURCE: H. Schwartz, *Russia's Soviet Economy* (New York: Prentice-Hall, Inc., 1950), pp. 222, 225, 332, 567, and 568.

(3) Specific indicators of output. The following table describes the output of individual producers' goods in the Soviet Union. The information available is very uneven and applies to different years. Table 3-9 attempts to make use of all information available; if one studied only those products whose output was reported in the same years, he would be restricted to very few commodities indeed.

The output of individual producers' goods shows the same general characteristics as the general indicators of output. Some items expanded enormously; a few basic products—specifically aluminum, tractors, grain combines, and motor vehicles—were produced for the first time in Russia by the Soviet government. Fundamental products like coal increased greatly in output—about ninefold; petroleum output increased over fourfold and pig iron production almost five times between 1913 and 1950. Basic chemicals, such as sulfuric acid, and fertilizers jumped greatly in output up to 1938, the last year for which information is available.

Table 3-10 shows the rise in the output of consumers' goods to be far less impressive than the increased output of producers' goods. The single most vital product, grain, increased between 1913 and 1950 by a smaller proportion than the population. (This statement takes account of the changed method of reporting grain output and the shift in boundaries after World War II.) A very great increase in potato output took place, however. "On balance, it seems clear that the amount of cereals, potatoes, and other crops used for human consumption in the Soviet Union is now somewhat greater *per capita* than in the same area before the first World War, but that this increase has been made possible in part by the relatively low level of livestock numbers over the last twenty years and has had as its apparent counterpart some decline in the *per capita* consumption of animal produce." [69]

The output of most industrial consumers' products seems to have outrun population growth, however. Also, we know that new consumers' products have been produced in considerable quantity for the first time under the Communist regime—specifically, radios, automobiles, electric refrigerators, and television sets.

There is no evidence to suggest that the Soviet Union has been exporting much of its output of industrial products to obtain consumers' goods. It has, if anything, exported consumers' goods in exchange for industrial equipment. Consequently, the reported output of consumers' goods does not understate the amount of goods available to the Soviet people.

[69] United Nations, Economic Commission for Europe, *Economic Bulletin for Europe,* Vol. 3, No. 2 (Geneva: October, 1951), p. 39.

TABLE 3-9

Output of Producers' Goods in the Soviet Union

Product	1913	Post-Civil War	Mid-1930's	1945	1952#	1955 goals
Coal*	29.1	7.2 ('20)	93.9 ('34)	149.3	300	373
Petroleum*	9.2	4.0 ('21)	24.2 ('34)	19.4	47	69.9
Pig iron*	4.2	0.1 ('20)	10.4 ('34)	9.2	25	34.1
Blister copper†	31,000	....	103,200 ('38)	...	291,000 ('51)	....
Electrolytic copper†	16,700	....	97,800 ('38)	...		
Lead‡	1,500	....	115,000 ('37 goal)	...		
Zinc†	2,900	....	90,000 ('37 goal)	...		
Aluminum†	0	0	57,000 ('38)	...		
Soda ash§	160	....	532 ('38)	...		
Sulfuric acid§	110	....	996 ('38)	...		
Fertilizers§	....	247 ('29)	2,610 ('38)	...	5,457 ('51)	9,600
Railroad main track‖	58.5	....	84.4 ('35)	112.9	118 ('49)	....
Motor vehicles#	....	1.4 ('29)	211.4 ('38)	83	405	486
Tractors#	0	1.3 ('27–'28)	116.1 ('36)	7.3	96	114.2
Grain combines#	0	0 ('27–'28)	42.6 ('36)	0.3	54††	....
Cement**	1.5	1.8 ('28)	5.7 ('38)	...	12.4††	22.9

* Million metric tons. † Metric tons. ‡ Tons. § Thousands of metric tons. ‖ Millions of kilometers. # Thousands. ** Millions of tons.

†† U.N. Economic Committee for Europe, *Economic Survey of Europe in 1951*, Table 2 (5), for the year 1951.

\# As reported in Malenkov's speech to Nineteenth Soviet Communist Party Congress.

SOURCE: H. Schwartz, *Russia's Soviet Economy* (New York: Prentice-Hall-Hall, Inc., 1950), selected pages, unless otherwise noted.

TABLE 3-10

Output of Selected Consumers' Goods and Services in the Soviet Union

Product	1913	Post–Civil War	Mid-1930's	1940	1945	1950
Grain production*	80.1	73.3 ('28)	90.1** ('35)	119**	66.5**	124**
Unginned cotton*	0.74	0.82 ('28)	2.58 ('37)	2.7	1.2	3.8
Sugar beets*	10.9	10.1 ('28)	21.9 ('37)	20.9	8.9	23.4
Fiber flax*	0.33	0.32 ('28)	0.57 ('37)	0.57	...	0.80
Hogs†	20.3	26.0 ('28)	17.4 ('34)	27.5 ('39)	10.4	....
Sheep and goats†	112	146.7 ('28)	51.9 ('34)	91.6 ('41)	69.4	99.0††
Cattle†	60.3	70.5 ('28)	42.4 ('34)	54.5 ('41)	47.0 ('46)	57.2††
Meat*	....	3.6 ('27–'28)	1.5 ('34)	3.3 ('38)	...	....
Cotton cloth‡	2,227 #	2,515 ('30)	2,612 ('35)	4,005	1,674	5,000§§
Woolen cloth‡	95 #	93.2# ('28)	114# ('38)	119.8	56.9	190§§
Leather shoes§ (large industry only)	....	29.6# ('28)	213# ('38)	220#	60	250§§
Hosiery§	....	208.0 ('32)	353.7 ('35)	480	83.0	430
Railroad passenger traffic‖	25.2	32.0 ('29)	67.9 ('35)	98.0	66.2	....

* Million metric tons. † Million heads. ‡ Million meters. § Million pairs. ‖ Billion passenger kilometers.

\# A. Baykov, *Industrial Development in the U.S.S.R.*, Bulletins on Soviet Economic Development, University of Birmingham, May, 1949, p. 8.

** Figures based on "standing crops" rather than crop harvests. This method of reporting raises the total. Agricultural output for various years is also not strictly comparable because of changes in the boundaries of the Soviet Union.

†† U.N. Economic Committee for Europe, *Economic Survey of Europe in 1951*, Table 5 (5).

§§ For 1952, as reported by Malenkov in his speech before the Nineteenth Soviet Communist Party Congress. Output goals for 1955 for cotton fabrics were 6,142; for woolen fabrics, 257; and for leather shoes, 318.

SOURCE: H. Schwartz, *Russia's Soviet Economy* (New York: Prentice-Hall, Inc., 1950), selected pages, unless otherwise noted.

The official index of industrial production by all industry in the Soviet Union shows a twelvefold increase.[70] This rise is larger than was observed in most products, though far smaller than in electric power generation, and not far out of line with some others like coal. While the Soviet index of industrial production is inflated, as Soviet statisticians admit, it nevertheless is not ridiculously out of line. Apparently Soviet planners have shifted away from stating goals in terms of 1926–1927 prices; it also is possible that indexes since 1950 are calculated in terms of prices in the period after World War II. A shift to the new index may account for the lower increase in industrial production between 1950 and 1951.

Although Soviet citizens apparently were given only slightly more consumers' goods by the Communist regime, they did obtain substantial gains in vital services. The quantity and quality of medical care increased greatly, as is shown in Table 3-11. By 1950, the number of doctors in the Soviet Union may have become almost ten times that of 1913, and hospital beds increased about five times during the same period.

In the decade of 1929 to 1939, enormous increases took place in educational and recreational facilities. The number of pupils in elementary and secondary schools more than doubled, students in universities and higher technical schools more than tripled; the number of public libraries kept pace with the rise in students. The number of theaters and motion-picture houses increased even more than the number of students and libraries.

Recent increases in cultural and social services have been as rapid as those before World War II. In 1950, 84 per cent more books were published than in 1940; clubs and libraries had increased by 15 per cent; there were 75 per cent more physicians in 1950 than in 1940. Over 5,000 new motion picture installations were made in 1950 alone.[71]

Levels of living in the Soviet Union are very low when compared with those in the United States. A delegation of British workers to the Soviet Union concluded that the standard of living of the

---

[70] A. Gerschenkron, "The Soviet Indices of Industrial Production," *Review of Economics and Statistics,* November, 1947, p. 218. This figure represents the goal of the fourth five-year plan, which was exceeded in 1950.

[71] "The Economic Superiority of Socialist Planning," *Monthly Review, An Independent Socialist Magazine,* September, 1951, p. 152.

TABLE 3-11
Social and Cultural Services in the Soviet Union

	1913	*1938*	*1941*	*1946*
Doctors	19,800	112,400	130,400	.....
Hospital beds	142,310	603,823	.....	694,000

	1929	*1933*	*1939*
Pupils (elem. and secondary schools in thousands)	12,068	21,398	31,517
Pupils (universities and higher technical schools in thousands)	177	504	603
Public libraries (thousands)	28.9	32.9	77.6
Theaters	153	551	787
Cinemas (thousands)	9.7	27.6	30.9

SOURCE: Adapted from Baykov, *The Development of the Soviet Economic System*, p. 347.

Soviet worker is close to that of the British worker,[72] though statistics on national income would indicate the British enjoy about a two-to-one advantage. One calculation puts the Soviet per capita income at about one fourth of that in the United States in 1949.[73]

The Russians themselves claim about a fourfold increase in the average standard of living in the Soviet Union since 1913. However, some foreign economic analysts deny that it has increased at all. The correct answer is difficult to discover because of the limited amount of information the Soviet Union will make available and because of the difficulty of defining living standards precisely. In the author's opinion, Soviet living standards increased only slightly between 1913 and, say, 1935. For a few years in the middle 1930's, living standards began to improve markedly, but this rise was brief, for the Russians intensified their armaments program when the likelihood of war became great. Living standards probably regained their prewar peak in about 1949, since which time they have risen fairly rapidly. The consumption of both food and manufactured goods has increased substantially, as price reductions have been

[72] *Russia with Our Own Eyes.* Full Official Report of the British Workers' Delegation to the Soviet Union, 1950 (New York: S.R.T. Publications, 1951), pp. 90–95.

[73] Prepared by the United Nations. See Table 2-6, pp. 42–43

made for broad groupings of consumers' goods while money incomes have continued to rise gradually.[74]

The rise in Soviet living standards was almost certainly smaller between 1913 and 1951 than the rise in American standards. Soviet claims of a fourfold increase are irreconcilable with the reported output of food, clothing, and housing. On the other hand, improvements in levels of living in the form of cultural services, medical care, vacations, and educational opportunities certainly have been great.

For the Soviet Union to have raised living standards more rapidly than it did would have required it to remain a weaker military power and to industrialize at a slower rate. The Soviet leaders, probably without the full support of the population, elected to build up the industrial potential of the country far more rapidly than living standards were improved. Presumably, the great increase in basic industries that has taken place in the Soviet Union will some day permit great increases in the output of consumers' goods. At this time, however, the Russian people must be satisfied with the knowledge that progress is being made in the basic industries instead of the reality of higher levels of living.

The following facts should be considered in interpreting the foregoing data. Population in the Soviet Union has increased substantially since the Communist Party gained control. Population in 1913 was 139 million, in 1926 147 million,[75] in 1940 198 million, and in 1950 about 205 million.[76] Accordingly, the number of persons who must be supported by the output of Soviet industry and agriculture has expanded considerably—albeit at a slower rate than the output of most products.

Moreover, the number of persons engaged in Soviet industry and agriculture has increased considerably since the Soviet regime took power. Part of the increased output observed, therefore, must be attributed to an increase in the number of persons engaged in productive activities.

Finally, the number of hours worked by Soviet citizens changed significantly at different times during the period studied.

---

[74] For a discussion of recent increases in supplies of consumers' goods and changes in their prices prepared by an anonymous source, see *Monthly Review,* September, 1951, pp. 148–154.

[75] Baykov, *The Development of the Soviet Economic System,* p. 122.

[76] A. Bergson, J. H. Blackman, and A. Erlich, "Postwar Economic Reconstruction and Development in the U.S.S.R.," *Annals of the American Academy of Political and Social Science,* May, 1949, p. 56.

In 1922, an eight-hour-day law was enacted; in April, 1927, a seven-hour working day was decreed. In September, 1929, the work week was altered; up to that time, employees worked six days in seven; after that date, they worked five days in six. This situation was changed on June 27, 1940, when the eight-hour day and six days' work in seven again became the rule.[77] Accordingly, Soviet workers enjoyed a shorter work day and work week up to 1940, and presumably some output gain that might have been attained was given up for the shorter work week. On the other hand, part of the increase in output since 1940 must be attributed to the increased number of hours worked.

2. *Noneconomic Characteristics of the Soviet Union*

Noneconomic goals have always figured prominently in Communist thinking. Accordingly, Soviet leaders have pursued many ends in addition to economic goals, and sometimes at a large sacrifice of economic achievements.

A] List of Major Noneconomic Achievements of the Soviet Union. The following achievements are relatively noncontroversial, though they are not universally acknowledged. They are presented in the form of a list in order to save space.

1. Russia has become a first-rate military power. She has used her power to acquire allies and has thereby enhanced her military security.

2. Interest in public affairs is keen, as evidenced by newspaper reading and attendance at political meetings and lectures.[78]

3. Russian agriculture has been reorganized and is now able to make efficient use of modern mechanized equipment.

4. Literacy has expanded enormously, from approximately 20 per cent in 1913 to about 90 per cent in 1950.

5. Notable advances have been made in pure and applied science, despite pressure on scientists to support an ideological line set down by the authorities.

6. Medical care of all types has been made freely available. Some criticism has been made of the quality of that care, however.

7. Soviet citizens who desire to work have been insured continuity of income, and thereby enjoy the pleasures of "security."

---

[78] Towster, *op. cit.*, p. 400.

[77] Baykov, *The Development of the Soviet Economic System*, pp. 140 and 351.

8. Cultural levels of the masses have been raised greatly and cultural facilities have been made generally available.

B] The Political System of the Soviet Union. To understand and evaluate the Soviet Union, its political character must be examined closely. Not all political systems would allow a government to industrialize such a poor country as the Soviet Union at so rapid a pace.

The Russians claim that their country is far more democratic than ours. Americans are certain that the truth is quite the other way around; indeed, we regard the Soviet Union as one of the clearest examples of dictatorship. So sharp a difference of opinion is unusual and is to be explained in several ways. First, and most important, we use the term "democracy" differently from the Russians. Second, no matter how the term "democracy" is defined, it is extremely difficult to assess the degree of democracy that exists in any country.

Americans tend to think that democracy exists if everyone can vote; where the right to vote is restricted, democracy is considered imperfect. By the test of pure "form," the Soviet Union is fully as democratic as the United States. Indeed, a far larger proportion of the adult population votes in the Soviet Union than in the United States. Moreover, to judge the degree of democracy in both countries by the basic rights and freedoms of citizens safeguarded by the constitution, the Soviet Union would seem to be the more democratic of the two. In addition to guarantees of freedom of speech and press, freedom of assembly, freedom of street processions and demonstrations, and the like, the Soviet constitution provides for "placing at the disposal of the working people and their organizations printing presses, stocks of paper, public buildings, the streets, communications facilities, and other material requisites for the exercise of these rights." (Article 125 of the 1936 constitution.) All of the freedoms guaranteed by the American constitution are also safeguarded by the Soviet constitution, which in addition outlaws infringements on personal liberty by restrictions on the rights of individuals on account of race or nationality, and punishes "advocacy of racial or national exclusiveness or hatred and contempt." (Article 123.) Clearly, the Soviet Union is *in form* a constitutional democracy of the most advanced type.

To define democracy in terms of form has little meaning, however. Our interest is in the substances of democracy. To determine the degree of substantive democracy is extraordinarily difficult, and rarely will many persons agree about the democracy of a specific country.

How would one define democracy in substantive terms? One author suggests that it refers "to the degree of response of government institutions and processes to the popular will." [79] This definition encounters a serious defect. Control over the mass means of propaganda makes it possible for a government to secure popular favor by deceiving the people. A majority of voters may freely vote in favor of the existing regime in ignorance of the fact that the government is incompetent, corrupt, and unmindful of the people's true interests. One might, therefore, define substantive democracy as a situation wherein the government does what a majority of well-informed people would favor as well as responds to the popular will. Of course, this definition is even more difficult to apply than one expressed solely in terms of responsiveness to the popular will.

Although one hears numerous assertions to the contrary, almost all newspapermen returning from the Soviet Union agree that there is relatively little dissatisfaction with the Soviet regime.[80] By the test of being in accord with the popular will, the Soviet Union is democratic. However, if a majority of individuals were of a mind to oust the government or to compel it to alter its basic policies, they would lack the means to do so. ". . . aside from a revolution, there is no means whereby the existing government can be replaced, nor is there any means of installing another party in place of the Communist Party." [81] Strong control over the press makes it very unlikely that the majority of people will ever become dissatisfied with the government in power. Nevertheless, Russians are not given the right to take political action in opposition to the Communist Party. "Assemblies which presumably are legislative meet to approve decisions made by more restricted bodies, which in turn approve decisions made by still smaller bodies, which eventually derive their policies from the Politburo—the innermost sanctum of the Communist Party." [82]

---

[79] Loucks and Hoot, *op. cit.,* p. 616.

[80] *Ibid.,* pp. 616–617, for recent examples, including statements by Brooks Atkinson of the *New York Times,* Carl W. McCardle of the *Philadelphia Evening Bulletin,* and C. L. Sulzberger of the *New York Times.*

[81] *Ibid.,* p. 619.

[82] *Ibid.*

Almost all American students of the problem are agreed that the Soviet state is not democratic. Whether or not the Communist Party, which rules the Soviet Union, is internally democratic is a more difficult question.[83] Professor Towster credits it with considerable democracy. He concludes that all members of the Politburo have equal voice, though Stalin's personal influence is great. "Differences of opinion can and do develop and Stalin has been outvoted on occasion," he reports.[84] On the other hand, Professor Schwartz declares that "there is no internal democracy in the Soviet state nor in the ruling Communist Party." [85]

The meaning of membership in the Communist Party is an important clue to the Soviet political system. Most persons in the party "give" to rather than "receive" from the nation. Members of the party are pledged to make special sacrifices for the furtherance of the state. Candidates for membership must meet rigorous tests. Membership prior to World War II "involved the most arduous obligations of a financial, service, and behavior nature. Besides an initiation fee, the member paid progressive rate dues to support party work. . . . Moreover, in motives, in sincerity, in effort, in performance, and even in the matter of personal consumption, party members were expected to set examples for other citizens, thus contributing to the ultimate goal of Communism. Even a suspicion that a member sought material advantage from his party status could result in loss of membership." [86]

The obligations of the highest leaders of the Soviet Union who are members of the Communist Party presumably are no smaller than those of rank and file members of the party. Members of the Politburo, for example, have assumed heavy obligations. Their be-

---

[83] The formal method of electing persons to office in the Soviet Union is as follows: (1) Candidates for high office are nominated by any public organization or society of working people, including a trade union, cooperative, youth organization, or the like. (2) Candidates nominated are narrowed down to one candidate for each office through nomination meetings attended by elected representatives of the various nominating bodies in that area. Each body is entitled to campaign for its nominee, but eventually the election commission for that area must certify one candidate for each post of deputy as the choice of the nominating bodies of that area. Adapted from Loucks and Hoot, *op. cit.*, p. 462. Thus the Soviet Union relies heavily on a device that is used by many organizations in the United States—the nominating committee that selects a slate that is almost invariably accepted by the rest of the membership in the election.

[84] Towster, *op. cit.*, p. 392.

[85] Schwartz, *op. cit.*, p. 95.

[86] Loucks and Hoot, *op. cit.*, p. 471.

havior is judged by high and harsh standards. Their purpose is taken to be the strengthening of Communism and the improvement of the condition of the working class. If they are truly motivated by a desire to serve the interests of the average citizen—which is a possibility that cannot be altogether dismissed—and also enjoy the support and affection of most of the people, the Soviet Union would possess vital ingredients of democracy. However, it would still fall far short of full political democracy, because the media of public expression are rigidly controlled by the government and because no peaceful means exist for replacing the current leaders.

Whereas Americans define democracy in terms of political procedures and rights, Communists ordinarily define democracy in economic terms. They apparently consider equality of economic opportunity the major element of democracy. To the extent that they attach importance to the average person's exerting an influence over government officials, they emphasize that the influence shall be exerted in matters that concern the individual directly—as in matters affecting his output norms and his general working conditions. They belittle the value of obtaining the general electorate's views on more remote matters, such as foreign policy and basic economic philosophy.

c] Attitudes and Personal Security under Communism. In our discussion of the noneconomic effects of capitalism, we noted primarily the creation of a materialistic outlook that contributes to personal unhappiness and feelings of personal insecurity. Does the Soviet economy directly or indirectly create similar conditions?

In the basic philosophical sense of the term, Communists accept the materialism espoused by Karl Marx. In the narrow sense in which the term is used here, the Communists are opposed to materialism. Public statements by the nation's leaders, teachings in the schools, literature, and other public media try to influence individuals to serve the nation and the general ideals of Communism. They clearly try to minimize the importance of worldly possessions. Indeed, many speak of Communism as a form of religion because, among other things, it calls for selfless devotion to a "cause." The Communists claim that Soviet citizens regard themselves as builders of a new and superior society. To the extent that this is true, and it is impossible to tell how true it is, Communism would give a satisfying purpose to life.

Personal insecurity in the United States is fundamentally economic. The danger of losing one's job or one's accumulated wealth due to an adverse turn in general business conditions or to a single error of one's own is the major cause of a feeling of insecurity. In the Soviet Union, unemployment—that is, the inability to obtain a job —is absent. (Unemployment sometimes arises from a lack of raw materials needed to carry on work, but workers are not fired and their incomes continue uninterrupted.) Thus, personal insecurity due to the threat of unemployment is almost absent in the Soviet Union. On the other hand, other types of insecurity may have been created (or continued from pre-Communist regimes) by the Communists. It has been argued that no Russian feels secure because he would be ruthlessly deprived of his personal freedom if he were so much as charged with opposition to the regime.

Soviet citizens who are strongly opposed to the existing system or to the rulers in power doubtless feel very insecure. Perhaps all persons who are prominently engaged in political activity recognize that they run a risk of pushing minority views too strongly and might come to be regarded as politically unreliable and receive harsh punishment as a result. We cannot tell, however, whether the *average* Soviet citizen, who, according to most reports, is loyal and behaves much as the nation's leaders would have him do, feels insecure. We simply do not know whether many citizens fear that they will be unjustly accused and punished. Professor Towster concluded that "the majority of Soviet citizens are not laboring under any undue sense of deprivation of freedom. . . . There is nothing to suggest that they are at present conscious of lacking the freedoms prevailing in the West." However, ". . . most of them, it can be reasonably assumed, would greatly welcome curtailment of the ubiquitous surveillance of the M.V.D." [87] (The M.V.D. is the Soviet secret service, and allegedly very harsh in its methods.)

D] Forced Labor in the Soviet Union. One of the most criticized features of the Soviet Union is its use of forced labor. It has been charged that the nation depends heavily upon forced labor and that its major achievements are mostly attributable to this source of manpower.[88] The number of forced laborers is variously estimated, some estimates putting the number over 20

---

[87] Towster, *op. cit.*, p. 386.

[88] See David J. Dallin, "The Slave Empire within the Soviet Empire," *New York Times* Sunday Magazine Section, October 14, 1951, p. 15.

million—about 10 per cent of the total population, and an even larger proportion of the adult population.

One wonders why the Soviet Union would favor forced labor over free labor. Forced labor generally is inefficient and wasteful. That is, a given group of workers will ordinarily produce more if they are working freely in response to positive incentives that elicit their voluntary efforts than if they work under threats and coercion. Consequently, one would expect the use of forced labor to lower output rather than to increase it. Although it would be necessary to pay free labor more than forced labor to perform unpleasant tasks, that fact is surely no obstacle to the Soviet authorities. They do not hesitate to pay very large wage differentials to those who do skilled work or who work in remote areas of the country. The use of free labor instead of forced labor to do unpleasant and dangerous jobs thus would both increase national output and redistribute it somewhat. The argument that the Soviet authorities prefer to use forced labor rather than free labor implies that they willingly forego increased output in order to save themselves the need of paying high wages to those who do dangerous and unpleasant work. This contention might be correct, but it is not particularly persuasive. When it is argued that the major achievements of the Soviet Union can be attributed to the use of forced labor, it becomes almost impossible to accept.

Soviet authorities say that forced labor camps are simply a type of prison and that people in these camps were convicted of nonpolitical as well as political crimes. Moreover, they deny that the number of prisoners is anywhere as large as charged. However, they do not indicate how many persons are in forced labor camps, and will not permit foreign observers to visit them.

It is clear that political offenders are put in forced labor camps. *Pravda* said in this connection: "All these criminals, from the landlords and capitalists down to the terrorists, thieves, assassins and subversive agents, are out to restore the exploitation of man by man and to drench the country in the blood of the workers and farmers. The prisons and labor camps exist for these gentlemen, and for them only." [89]

Soviet forced labor camps differ from prisons in the United States in that the inmates are employed at tasks similar to those per-

[89] *New York Times,* August 1, 1951.

formed by free labor and are paid for these services. Living conditions apparently are extremely hard in many instances. It is charged that forced labor camps suffer from very high death rates and that sanitation is crude.

It is impossible to estimate accurately the number of persons in forced labor camps. It is possible to learn, especially from people who have been released or have escaped from such camps, about their existence and location. It is quite another matter to estimate the number of persons in them. Camps seem to be moved from place to place so that the inmates can work on new projects; consequently, the same camp may be counted several times. Some camps, on the other hand, may never come to the attention of the outside world. Only a few people know how many forced laborers there are, and these are high Soviet officials. They have not told the world what they know. The numbers that are bandied about are sometimes honest estimates; quite as often, they are wholly unfounded.

The number of people in forced labor camps is especially interesting, for it would suggest the proportion of the Soviet population that is regarded as politically dangerous at this relatively late date. However, we are not likely to find out how many there are.

In the present discussion, therefore, the issue concerning forced labor camps is primarily whether they are simply a type of prison, different from our own prisons only in the sociological theories of criminal therapy upon which they are based, or whether they are an important and necessary element in the Soviet economy. Experience suggests that forced labor represents a loss rather than a gain in total output and productivity. In other words, the inmates of forced labor camps would produce more out of labor camps than in them. The significance of these camps seems to be noneconomic. They may be proof—if they contain many recent political prisoners—that, even after three decades of Soviet rule, popular dissatisfaction with the Soviet regime is widespread.

Up to this point, the noneconomic characteristics of the Soviet Union and its political system have been described. We have not yet inquired whether these are necessarily related to detailed economic planning, or are due to factors extraneous to the Soviet type of economic system. Put simply, does detailed economic planning necessarily result in dictatorships and forced labor? Does it always seek to raise cultural standards and expand medical care and education? These questions cannot be answered on the basis of Soviet experience alone; it would be even more difficult to answer them solely on the basis of speculation.

The author does not believe there is a *necessary* connection between detailed economic planning and dictatorship. (Dictatorship, however, is indispensable if the rulers want to industrialize at a very rapid rate when living levels are low.) In his opinion, there is still reason to hope, though one cannot confidently expect, that the Soviet Union will become increasingly democratic in the Western sense of the term. If that ever happens, it will come only after the Soviet Union has achieved what it regards as military security and a fairly high standard of living.

IX. CONCLUSIONS

Clearly the Soviet Union is unique and complex. It has undergone considerable change under a Communist regime that has shown a readiness to experiment; it may develop along unexpected lines.

The Soviet Union has demonstrated that a detailed planned economy can survive under Communist leadership. Moreover, Russia was transformed from a nation that had been a third-rate power into a great world power whose military might is feared even by the United States.

As yet, the achievements of the Soviet Union leave in serious doubt the suitability of detailed planning for nations that already have high living standards. Moreover, the issue of whether detailed economic planning requires dictatorship is at best unsettled; there are very few signs of increased personal liberties or a removal of restraints on expressions of adverse opinions about basic philosophy. Apparently the Communist Party in the Soviet Union is resolved to retain the present arrangements, no matter what the majority views of the people may be.

Most striking about the Soviet Union is its detailed economic planning. It seems that the planners decide vital matters quite arbitrarily and accordingly are in danger of making important mistakes. However, the means for correcting errors also exist. While planning procedures have improved since the Communists took power, existing procedures seem to fall far short of perfection.

The Soviet Union is conducting an interesting economic experiment. To hope for the downfall of a new economic system *in another nation* just because it is different from ours or we think it inferior to ours does not make sense. The opposition in the United States to the Soviet Union cannot be traced to sympathy for the Russian people. The clash of American and Soviet policies and ideologies stems mainly from other causes, particularly from American opposition to the expansion of Communism over the world by the use of political pressure or military force. One should not identify detailed economic planning with an expansionist foreign policy. In this discussion of the Soviet Union, an attempt was made to examine the Soviet economy separately from its foreign policy. On the other hand, in their dealings with the Soviet Union, our officials must give primary attention to its foreign policy. Whatever our attitude toward Soviet foreign policy, we can learn a great deal about the benefits and shortcomings of detailed economic planning by following carefully the development of the Soviet economy.

CHAPTER FOUR

The Economy of the United Kingdom

The economies of the United States and the Soviet Union represent extremes. Government participation in the first is relatively slight, while it pervades the latter. In 1945, when the Labor Party was voted into power, the United Kingdom began an experiment with a "middle way" between these extremes. Even after the defeat of the Labor Party in October, 1951, the British economy continues to occupy middle ground between the American and Soviet economic systems.

It is difficult to describe and analyze the British economy for several reasons. First, it does not rest on any clear-cut body of doctrine. The principles and philosophy underlying British public policy are undergoing thorough reformulation.[1] As a result of the drastic change in her international position, the big drop in her income from abroad, and the impact of the war, a profound re-examination of fundamental economic conceptions is taking place in the United Kingdom.

Second, the balance of political power in the United Kingdom is very delicate. As this is written, the major party in Parliament is Conservative. That party took power with a slim parliamentary majority, won with fewer popular votes than were given the Labor Party. It remains to be seen whether the Conservatives continue most of the measures enacted by the Labor Party, as they promised, or whether they make substantial changes in the economy.

The following discussion rests upon the author's belief that the British economy reflects the philosophy, objectives, and principles of the Labor Party. If the Conservative Party strengthens its parliamentary majority, it will presumably modify the economy in the di-

[1] For example, Professor J. E. Meade begins his book *Planning and the Price Mechanism* (New York: The Macmillan Company, 1949) as follows: "The basic principles of our economic policy are once more in the melting pot."

rection of the American system. In the near future, however, no substantial modification can be anticipated. Upon taking control of Parliament in October, 1951, the Conservative Party filled the chief post in the Cabinet concerned with domestic economic affairs with a man who is an outspoken exponent of the welfare state—Chancellor of the Exchequer R. A. Butler.

The goals, principles, and philosophy of the Labor Party are stressed in discussing the present British economy both because the present economy reflects the philosophy of the Labor Party and, perhaps more important, because no matter what happens to the British economy in the future, the six years under Labor Party control form a highly illuminating chapter in recent history.

I. BASIC CHARACTERISTICS OF THE BRITISH ECONOMY

At least until October, 1951, most Americans described the British economy as "socialistic." Indeed, the platform on which the Labor Party fought the election campaign of 1945 explicitly stated: "The Labor Party is a Socialist Party and proud of it."[2] However, the British economy diverges widely from socialism as that term is ordinarily used. It is more accurately described as a "welfare state" or a "controlled economy."

There is considerable disagreement about the fundamental character of the British economy. Because it has been undergoing substantial modification since 1945, it can be interpreted in various ways. Moreover, some people judge it by the statements of public officials rather than by existing arrangements.[3] It nevertheless is generally agreed that the United Kingdom represents a unique combination of economic arrangements. While it has imitated some control measures employed in Sweden, Denmark, New Zealand, and Australia, it has modified those it has borrowed and in addition has adopted new measures. Great Britain represents the only highly industrialized country to employ a welfare economy.

---

[2] "Let Us Face the Future," program statement by the British Labor Party, 1945, Sec. IV, published by the Labor Party Office (London: April, 1945).

[3] Even though, as Dr. E. Sikes points out in *Contemporary Economic Systems* (New York: Henry Holt & Company, 1951, p. 166), ". . . rarely if ever did a party carry out its program so completely as did Labour in the four and one half years between its coming to office and the election of 1950," the British economy did not realize the *long-range* goals of the leaders of the Labor Party.

To illuminate the fundamental characteristics of the present British economy, the principles underlying the Labor government's program, its major objectives, and the specific measures employed to achieve its stated goals will be discussed separately.

A] PRINCIPLES UNDERLYING THE LABOR GOVERNMENT'S PROGRAM

While it is avowedly socialistic, the Labor Party is emphatically not doctrinaire. Its political support comes from a wide variety of economic groups holding diverse views; few of these groups have a carefully worked out political philosophy.

The Labor Party draws its political support from four major groups that partly overlap: the trade-union movement, the cooperative societies, the intellectual socialists, and the advocates of economic planning. The trade unions represent the strongest single group of supporters by far. At present, the dominant personalities in the leadership of the British trade-union movement and, therefore, highly influential in the Labor Party, are men, "shrewd, hard driving, essentially opportunistic, earthy, practical, and contemptuous of ideas, ideologies, theories, and social philosophies." [4] The supporters of the Labor Party from the cooperative societies have a general economic philosophy, but it does not cover most of the matters with which a government must deal. Only the doctrinaire socialists, a relatively small group, have a well-integrated political philosophy; on occasion the Labor Party is compelled to make concessions to hold the support of that group. A fourth major group that has supported the Labor Party is comprised of those people who had been impressed with the benefits of economic planning during World War II and became convinced that it could also go far to solve peacetime economic problems.

Professor Brady, after a very careful and searching diagnosis of the Labor Party's program, states that the British Labor government proceeded "undogmatically" and employed a ". . . practical . . . empirical . . . and experimental approach." The Party ". . . is held to be free of any definite commitment to any clear-cut theory." He concludes that one cannot even infer a theory from the statements and activities of the British Labor Party, whose program he regards as a highly unstable set of compromises.[5]

---

[4] Robert Brady, *Crisis in Britain* (Berkeley: University of California Press, 1950), pp. 30–31.

[5] *Ibid.*, pp. 33–34.

Perhaps the fundamental characteristic of the Labor Party's political principles is to be found in its attitude toward the function of government. It regards government participation in economic affairs as benign under most circumstances, rather than as an evil to be almost always avoided. Nevertheless, it does not regard government regulation or control as "good in itself"; for example, after World War II, it removed wartime controls with considerable speed.

The Laborites describe the difference between their attitude toward government and that of the Conservatives in the following terms. Their opponents, the Laborites claim, say, "'Full employment. Yes! If we can get it without interfering too much with private industry.' We say, 'Full employment in any case, and if we need to keep a firm public hand on industry in order to get jobs for all, very well.'"[6] The Labor government does not regard restriction of private industry's activities as wrong in itself and would presumably resort to it whenever it felt that the economy's performance would be improved thereby. (The Conservative Party does not necessarily accept the Labor Party's version of its views.)

B] OBJECTIVES OF THE LABOR GOVERNMENT

Labor's program is directed toward far more than economic goals. Insofar as its goals are economic, it pursues economic security and high living standards as means toward a higher goal. Specifically, this higher goal is ". . . the evolution of a people more kindly, intelligent, free, cooperative, enterprising, and rich in culture. They are means to the greater end of the full and free development of every individual person."[7]

The specific economic objectives for which the British Labor government aimed are quite clear. The paramount aims, once the physical and financial damage incurred during World War II was repaired, were, first, to carry forward a vigorous defense program; second, to equalize personal incomes by means of taxes and welfare expenditures; third, to stabilize employment; fourth, to increase output by means of improvements in productive efficiency. The first objective is common to all political parties in the United Kingdom and arises from the particular setting in which Great Britain finds herself. Labor's measures for meeting this problem indicated

[6] "Let Us Face the Future," Sec. III.

[7] "Let Us Win Through Together," British Labor Party Election Manifesto in 1950.

little about the party's long-range program. Our attention, therefore, will be concentrated on the manner in which the last three objectives were pursued.

C] MEASURES FAVORED BY THE LABOR GOVERNMENT

The Labor Party offers no panacea for correcting the shortcomings of the British economy. Within its membership are doctrinaire socialists who, like socialists everywhere, hold that nationalization will cure virtually all economic ills. Most Laborites, however, are prepared to experiment and improvise. The specific measures that figured most prominently in the Labor government's program will become clear as we discuss the major parts of that program. These control measures comprise a long list.[8]

Before the workings of the British economy are explored, the setting in which the Labor Party took power will be discussed briefly. Thereafter, the manner in which it sought to equalize personal incomes, to plan for long-range economic development and for full employment, the role of nationalization in its program, and its efforts to increase productivity will be considered in detail.

II. SETTING IN WHICH THE LABOR GOVERNMENT TOOK POWER

As already indicated, most of the Labor government's past actions were responses to circumstances beyond its control—resulting primarily from World War II and the need to guard against possible Russian aggression. The Labor government, moreover, inherited an economy when it took office in which many major industries had become unprogressive and were using out-of-date plant and equipment. Also, the Labor government's program was guided at least in part by the desire to hold its original political support and to gain new supporters.[9] Consequently, it was limited in the extent to which it could carry out its long-range program. Rather than a government single-mindedly devoted to the reform of the economic

---

[8] "Controls in the United Kingdom," prepared by the British Embassy, January 24, 1951, distributed by British Information Services.

[9] While the Laborites held a large parliamentary majority after the 1945 election, they obtained less than a majority of the popular vote. In the 1950 election, they lost only slight popular support, but their parliamentary majority became exceedingly slender.

system, the Labor government was forced to dedicate itself primarily to immediate economic recovery and rearmament, and to be extremely mindful of political realities. One can only guess what the Laborites would have done once recovery and rearmament were completed and they were assured of political support.

The magnitude of the reconstruction problem faced by Great Britain at the end of World War II is indicated by the war losses listed below.[10]

1. Property actually destroyed as a result of military action—mostly by bombing and sinking of merchant marine: estimated at $9.9 billion.

2. British overseas investments liquidated to finance purchases during the war and overseas debt incurred for the same reason: estimated at £6 billion (about $24 billion).[11]

3. Depreciation of plant and equipment that was not made good during the war: estimated to be approximately $10 billion.

4. Manpower losses: 600,000 men dead or wounded.

Due to these types of economic damage, the direct productive power of the United Kingdom was impaired and its claims against the output of foreign countries declined.[12] A substantial decline in British living conditions below prewar levels was therefore almost inevitable.

Moreover, following World War II, Great Britain lost control over important parts of her empire. The greatest loss was India. Burma also loosened her ties with the United Kingdom; and virtually ever since the end of World War II, the British have been fighting to maintain control of Malaya. In various and subtle ways, the loss of these territories has reduced Britain's overseas income.

Britain's difficulties at the end of World War II were substantially aggravated by the adverse movement in terms of trade. The world shortage of most foods and raw materials after the war raised the prices of these goods far more than the prices of the manufac-

---

[10] Based primarily on Brady, *op. cit.*, pp. 5–6.

[11] A detailed analysis of the timing and the countries involved in Britain's changed overseas investments and liabilities is presented in "Britain's Overseas Investments and Liabilities," British Information Services, April, 1951.

[12] These claims arose as a result of the investments in foreign countries held by British citizens. Income on overseas investments prior to World War II paid for approximately 20 per cent of total British imports. See *Britain 1950–51, A Reference Handbook* (London: Central Office of Information, October, 1950), p. 61.

tures that Britain exports. In 1948 about one fifth more goods had to be exported than in 1938 to bring in the same quantity of imports.[13]

Even before World War II damaged the British production machine, the United Kingdom's economy showed a marked decline in vitality. Compared with plant and equipment in the United States, many major British industries were admittedly out of date. (Some, mainly the newer light manufacturing industries, did keep pace with the United States and Germany.) British industrialists were slow to enter new markets, to adopt new techniques of production, and to experiment with modern marketing methods. They devoted considerable effort, instead, to restrictionist schemes for dividing domestic and foreign markets. Due to the virtually uninterrupted depression between the two world wars, industrialists and the government were not anxiously concerned about raising output. They believed that increased prosperity would come from the prevention of "excessive competition."

Similarly, most British labor unions opposed improvements in productive technique. They too were concerned with protection against "excessive competition" for jobs. (Rather than desiring increased output, they thought reduced output would give them, individually, higher living standards.)

In addition to the reduced productivity of the British economy, and partly as a result of that decline, the United Kingdom lost some of its foreign markets to Germany and the United States. In addition, she lost some foreign markets because of the spread of industrialization in many parts of the world to which she sold. The dollar shortage, about which so much has been heard since World War II, already had started before the war began.[14]

Like most other governments that promise a drastic change, the Labor Party took office under extremely difficult conditions. Since it is firmly pledged to political democracy, it was compelled to adopt measures that would retain its political support at every step of the way; otherwise it would have had no opportunity to carry its program forward. Consequently, most of its program consisted of a series of compromises in which immediate recovery rather than a reform of the economy received first attention. (Socialists the world over still debate whether the Laborites should have

[13] *Ibid.*

[14] S. Enke and V. Salera, *International Economics* (New York: Prentice-Hall, Inc., 1951), p. 642.

undertaken a drastic program of socialization immediately and thereby have shown the people that they were sincere and energetic. It is doubtful that the Labor Party could have moved faster and farther and still have managed creditably the parts of the economy it undertook to manage. Greater speed of socialization, the author believes, would have required a suspension of democratic elections for a considerable period.)

III. THE LONG-RANGE PROGRAM OF THE LABOR GOVERNMENT

The Labor Party's major long-range objectives included: (1) equalization of personal income; (2) long-range development and full employment by means of economic planning; (3) nationalization; (4) increases in productive efficiency. These objectives could be pursued in a variety of ways. Let us examine the means by which the British Labor government tried to achieve these ends.

A] EQUALIZATION OF PERSONAL INCOMES

Under its "fair shares" program, the Labor government sought to equalize income distribution by its tax and expenditure policy. It achieved far more in this direction by its expenditure policy than by its tax program. Heavy and progressive income taxes equalized money incomes to a considerable degree even before World War II. (See Table 4-1.)

1. *Tax Policy*

Under the Labor government, personal income taxes, corporate profits taxes, and indirect taxes (mostly taxes on consumption) were increased. The tax increases were made largely, if not entirely, to combat strong inflationary pressures. Indirect taxes on consumption were almost as great as personal income and corporate profits taxes combined in 1949.[15] These indirect taxes are not intended to redistribute income; indeed, they tend to accentuate rather than reduce the inequality of real income.

Changes in income tax rates under the Labor government did

[15] Specifically, personal income taxes yielded £1,307 million and corporate profits taxes £721 million; indirect taxes on consumption contributed revenue of £1,971 million. See *Britain 1950–1951*, p. 67.

equalize income distribution somewhat (Tables 4-1 and 4-2). Moreover, under the Labor government the share of the total national income received from wage payments increased significantly, while income from salaries and profits, interest, and rent declined (Table 4-3).

Table 4-2 makes clear that considerable income redistribution had taken place under the Conservatives in 1938. It was greater, for example, than the redistribution of personal income in 1949 in the United States.[16] Under the Labor Party, income redistribution was pushed further. In 1949, the very prosperous people in Britain received an insignificant part of the national income—about one half of 1 per cent.[17]

TABLE 4-1

Personal Incomes in the United Kingdom after Taxes, 1938–1939, 1947–1948

Range of net income	Number of individuals	
	1938–1939	1947–1948
£120–£150		2,030,000
150– 250	4,500,000	8,470,000
250– 500	1,820,000	8,740,000
500–1,000	450,000	1,378,000
1,000–2,000	155,000	320,000
2,000–4,000	56,000	58,500
4,000–6,000	12,000	3,430
Over 6,000	7,000	70
Total	7,000,000	21,000,000

SOURCE: *British Economic Record,* British Information Services, February 28, 1950, p. 2.

[16] Tables 2-2 and 2-3.

[17] Even if one draws the line at incomes over £2,000 (roughly $5,600) instead of £10,000, only 5.5 per cent of all income after taxes went to prosperous persons. In evaluating the effect of taxation upon income distribution, attention must be given to the conventions regarding tax payments and the efficiency of tax collections. It is said that tax evasions and "avoidance" are far less usual in the United Kingdom than in the United States.

TABLE 4-2

Personal Incomes in the United Kingdom by Income Classes, 1938, 1949
(As a per cent of total personal income)

Income classes	1938		1949	
	Pretax	Posttax	Pretax	Posttax
Under £250	59.2	63.7	24.5	27.5
£250–£499	14.6	15.2	39.2	42.3
500– 999	8.4	8.0	17.8	17.3
1,000–1,999	5.7	5.0	8.0	6.8
2,000–9,999	8.4	6.4	8.4	5.5
10,000 and over	3.7	1.7	2.1	0.6
Total	100.0	100.0	100.0	100.0

SOURCE: Calculated from data in absolute amount from *National Income and Expenditure of the U.K., 1946–50,* Command 8203.

TABLE 4-3

Personal Income after Direct Taxes According to Source

Source of income	Percentage of total income received	
	1938–1939	1947–1948
Wages	39%	48%
Salaries	25	21
Profits, interest, and rent	34	28

SOURCE: *British Economic Record,* British Information Services, February 28, 1950, p. 2.

The information presented in Tables 4-1 and 4-3 is not easily interpreted. The 1938–1939 data exclude the incomes of the large number of persons whose incomes were less than £150 because they were not compelled to report their incomes to the government. Only 7 million personal incomes are reported for the early period, and three times as many for 1947–1948. Consequently, the 1938–1939 figures fail to indicate the very large proportion of income recipients whose incomes were below £150. In addition, one must take into account the substantial rise in cost of living that took place between the early and late period, which amounted to about 85 per cent. Accordingly, the number of very large *real* incomes in recent years is smaller than the table suggests. Third, it is impossible to determine to what extent the Conservatives would have been compelled to redistribute personal income by means of taxation to cover the unavoidably high expenditures of the government.

A very large proportion of all tax income in the United Kingdom comes from direct levies on the sale of drink and tobacco. In 1950, for example, excise taxes on these two products yielded revenue of £1 billion.[18] Accordingly, the tax burden of any consumer must be calculated with direct reference to his purchases of the heavily taxed items like tobacco, alcoholic beverages, and gasoline. A careful study of the British tax program led to this conclusion: "The benefits of (income) redistribution cut across income groups and are largely related to consumption."[19] The taxes on certain items that are purchased by low income groups have been increased to pay for some of the services distributed freely to low income recipients.

Taxes of all kinds accounted for 41 per cent of private income received in 1948 and 1949. (Even before the war, tax revenues in the United Kingdom took a very large proportion of the total national income; for example, in 1938 taxes represented 24 per cent of total income.) These high tax revenues, motivated partly by the desire to redistribute personal income, apparently have not had an adverse effect on total output. Mr. Weaver concludes that taxation has not prevented a rise in output or a movement toward lower costs. Indeed, rises in production and productivity appear to have been as great in the United Kingdom as in the United States between the end of World War II and 1950.[20]

The big improvement in the position of the wage earner (Table 4-3) is due almost entirely to full employment rather than to the preferential tax position of wage earners.[21] The burden of unemployment fell disproportionately upon workers; hence they gained most from the high employment levels following the war.

---

[18] *Economic Survey for 1951,* Command 8195 (London: April, 1951), p. 43.

[19] Findley Weaver, "Taxation and Redistribution in the United Kingdom," *The Review of Economics and Statistics,* August, 1950, p. 201.

[20] *Ibid.*

[21] *Ibid.,* pp. 206 and 212.

Income distribution was also influenced indirectly by the rise in corporate profits taxes under the Labor government. As indicated, corporate profits taxes contributed more than half as much revenue in 1949 as personal income taxes. The present rate of tax on corporate profits varies between 53 and 66 per cent, depending on the proportion of profits distributed.[22] (Recipients of dividends do not have to pay income tax on the dividends a second time.) In 1938, corporate profits were taxed at a rate of 27.5 per cent.

2. *Welfare Services in Income Equalization*

The Labor government equalized personal incomes by means of its welfare expenditures, rather than by its tax program. Highly progressive income taxation need not redistribute personal income. If the proceeds of taxation are spent in ways that help only those who pay the taxes, real income is not redistributed. In the United Kingdom a large proportion of government expenditures gives poor people more than they pay in taxes.

It is difficult to define welfare services. From one point of view, everything done by a government can be considered a welfare service. The only justification for any government expenditure is that it contributes to the nation's welfare. However, welfare services usually denote special kinds of government services—specifically, social insurance, health services, housing and food subsidies, subsidies to education, children's allowances and lunches, and the like. All these services have one essential characteristic in common: they are believed to be necessary for the survival, progress, and moral health of the nation; accordingly, they are extended without charge or at substantially less than cost on the basis of need.

It is roughly estimated that the average British family gets welfare services whose value is one fifth of its money income. The major components of the income received from welfare services are to be seen in an analysis of the expenditures by the British government. In assessing the quantitative importance of these welfare services, the following figure should be used as a point of reference. In 1949, the total British population spent for personal consumption £8.4 billion. During that year, the following expenditures were made for the designated welfare services:

[22] British Information Services, *United Kingdom Income Tax,* I.D. 729, April, 1951, pp. 3-4.

	(In thousands of pounds)
Food subsidies, including acreage payments	£ 403
National Health Service	374
Assistance to local governments for education	243
Family allowances	62
Contributions to social insurance systems	152
Assistance to local governments for housing	61
Central government housing subsidies	24
Local housing subsidies	51
Total	£1,370

Included in the above, though possibly not made clear by the terms used, are welfare foods for children, including school milk, vitamin foods; school meals for all children in public schools; old-age, sickness, and unemployment insurance; and maternity and death benefits. Not included are a large number of general services and subsidies that raise the total to almost £2 billion.[23]

The importance of these expenditures is to be found primarily in their psychological effect. They provide the average person with insurance against life's greatest financial hazards—though only to a minimum degree, it should be noted—and afford an opportunity for individuals to rise in economic class. Their effect on the willingness of workers to accept changes in production techniques, the personal pleasure with which people do their work, and the like, represent their true importance; but these things cannot be measured.

Clearly, by a combination of tax policy and welfare expenditures, personal income distribution was substantially equalized by the Labor government. Considerable variation in personal incomes still remained when it was voted from power, however. The performance of the economy in the face of income equalization suggests that productive incentive was not greatly impaired, if at all, in the process.

B] ECONOMIC PLANNING IN THE UNITED KINGDOM

The degree to which the British economy was planned under the Labor government is a matter of some dispute. Some British economists refer to the economy under Labor as essentially one of "free enterprise," while others say it was hog-tied with government

[23] Data on expenditures are from *Britain, 1950–51,* pp. 75–76.

regulations and plans. Certainly, the Labor government employed far less economic planning than the Soviet Union; it is quite as certain that it planned the operations of the economy far more than is done in the United States.

Economic planning initiated by the Labor government was directed fundamentally toward the stabilization of the economy at nearly full employment and toward long-term industrial and regional development. An understanding of planning in Great Britain under the Labor government will be sought by analysis of the governmental machinery for planning that was erected, the manner in which full employment was to be sought, and the means by which long-range development was planned. First, however, let us see what place the Labor Party intended planning to hold in its long-range program.

1. *Role of Economic Planning in the Labor Party Program*

According to the former Adviser on Public Relations to the Prime Minister and a close and working companion of the top leaders of the Labor Party, it was decided that the government "must proceed by joint consultation with managements and trade unionists. It cannot employ the compulsions that totalitarian planning uses, nor would it wish to do so." [24] "There remains and must remain under a democratic socialistic system a large area of the national economy where influence can be exercised only by discussion and persuasion; . . . Moreover, the British socialist experiment is designed to produce an economic pattern in which only a portion of industry—although the most basic portion—will be directly owned and controlled by the public, while the rest, although subject to social control, will be conducted by private enterprise in order to secure a partnership between individual initiative and social planning . . ."[25] It thus appears that the Labor Party hoped to create an economy that is "planned to a degree." The precise degree to which planning would ultimately have been undertaken if the Laborites had remained in office for a long time is quite unclear. To judge from their general philosophy, it would depend upon the amount needed to attain the major objectives of full employment and equalization of incomes; beyond that point they would leave a maximum

[24] Francis Williams, *Socialist Britain* (New York: The Viking Press, Inc., 1949), p. 87.

[25] *Ibid.*, pp. 88–89.

degree of freedom for businessmen, consumers, and laborers. With this philosophy, the Laborites might have ended up with a thoroughly planned economy, or one that differed from ours only in small degree. At the time the Labor government was voted out of office, the British economy was far more like ours than like that of the Soviet Union.

2. *Machinery for Planning*

During the first few years after it took office, the British Labor government failed to create new machinery for general economic planning. Only the controls that had been established during the war were employed. In September, 1947, however, in response to growing recognition that little "over-all" planning was being done, the skeleton of a planning organization was created. Under this arrangement, economic planning was to be carried out by the Cabinet; a Minister of Economic Affairs was to be personally responsible for economic planning. Two committees were made responsible to the Minister of Economic Affairs. One of them, known as the Central Economic Planning Staff, composed of top civil servants, collected economic data for the preparation of the annual Economic Survey, describing the broad economic developments of the recent past and projecting in broad terms the desired developments of the near future. The work of this staff was to provide most of the information upon which the Cabinet made its decisions. The second committee engaged in economic planning, also responsible to the Minister of Economic Affairs, was the Economic Planning Board. This group was composed of management, labor, and government representatives, and served purely in an advisory capacity.

By 1949, there was no lack of administrative machinery for the performance of economic planning. In practice, however, ". . . most of the planning is actually done by individual government departments or by inter-departmental committees." [26] Most planning occurred only on rather a low level, and largely concerned individual industries, single geographical regions, or a single raw material. Economic plans in which all parts of the economy were fitted into the total economic picture apparently existed primarily in the form of the Economic Surveys.

Of course, officials concerned with specific problems on a medium or low level were encouraged to take into account broad na-

[26] *Business Week,* March 18, 1950, p. 58.

tional considerations. Frequently, individual planning groups sought advice from persons concerned with the total national problem. However, the Labor Party's planners never prepared a picture of the kind of economy they hoped to create that would have guided individuals in deciding specific matters as they arose.

Before one judges how much economic planning is ultimately intended by the Labor Party, he should recall that, when it was in power, it was dedicated primarily to solving short-run problems. A large proportion of England's skilled administrators and economists were engaged in meeting immediate problems. Only when these persons could have been shifted to longer-range problems could the Labor government have succeeded with more ambitious types of planning. Over-all planning is extremely complicated and time consuming, and at best could not have been expected to develop quickly.

A few of the wartime controls that the Labor government inherited permitted a significant type of general economic planning. By far the most important governed the allocation of steel, timber, and building licenses. These controls enabled the Labor government to expand and to contract individual industries using basic productive factors. Presumably, decisions about the allocation of basic resources were made with the "total picture" of the economy in view. Consequently, these controls permitted *general* as distinct from *specific* planning.

3. *Planning for Full Employment*

To maintain relatively full employment, the Labor government would have used a variety of measures, chief of which are control over total expenditure and direct control over investment. These measures are closely related, inasmuch as investment is the most variable type of expenditure; if it were stabilized, major dips in employment should not occur.

The Economic Survey prepared by the Central Economic Planning Staff set forth the proportion of the national income that "should be" devoted to investment. ". . . the government can by no means, within the framework of the socialist plan as envisaged in Britain, compel all industries to produce exactly what is required of them." [27] However, by a variety of measures, the Labor government

[27] Williams, *op. cit.*, p. 88.

could have strongly influenced the total volume of investment and even its industrial composition.

First, it could directly influence expenditures by government—including, in addition to the usual type of government expenditure, investment expenditure by nationalized industries. Second, it regulated the issues of securities (over some small size) for the purpose of financing new investment through its Capital Issues Committee. This agency could influence total investment primarily in a negative way; that is, it could prevent firms from borrowing, but it could not compel them to borrow. It could determine the industries in which private investment might take place by permitting some to issue securities but denying others that privilege. Third, the government could influence both total investment and its industrial composition through its allocation of basic materials among alternative applicants. Fourth, the government had power to license the purchases of scarce industrial equipment; its licensing policy influenced the rate at which equipment was purchased. Fifth, the government was given the power in some instances to subsidize capital expenditures to modernize an inefficient industry.[28]

Outside its own budget expenditures and subsidy policy, the Labor government could not directly initiate capital investment. It could only select among those private industries that desired to invest. Thus, its power to restrict investment expenditure was far greater than its power to increase it. In the long run, insufficient private investment may be a greater problem than excessive investment.

In the event that its control over investment proved insufficient to maintain full employment, the Labor government could have taken measures to increase consumer expenditure. Its social security program would have gone a long way toward stabilizing consumer expenditure; however, if necessary, the Labor government would have reduced personal income taxes and, in extreme cases, even made outright grants of funds to employed persons to increase their expenditures.

Due to the large demands generated by the need to repair war damage and the inflationary effects of the defense program, the British Labor government's ability to prevent unemployment was not put to the test.

[28] Brady, *op. cit.*, p. 549.

4. *Planning for Long-Range Development*

Long-range planning in the United Kingdom under Labor was concerned primarily with the following problems: reorganization and modernization of industry, expansion of agricultural output, and industrial relocation. The first problem will be discussed presently in connection with the analysis of nationalization and of efforts to make private industry more productive; the agricultural program will be mentioned briefly in passing when miscellaneous government controls are discussed. The discussion here will primarily concern the location of new plants and the relocation of old ones.

Great Britain has suffered severely because the industrial composition of many areas has not been diversified; large regions have been dependent upon activity in a single industry. When that industry experienced cyclical unemployment or, worse still, began to decline, the population of that region suffered acutely. In addition to aiming for diversification of industry, long-range plans were directed toward locating industry in a way that would make most efficient use of natural resources, existing public utility services, and available labor supplies. Three instruments were used to achieve these objectives: the Distribution of Industry Act, which permitted the government to lend money to "trading estates," to give financial assistance to concerns that opened factories in designated areas and built factories to be owned by the government but leased to private owners at low rentals; the building licensing system, under which no new factories were built anywhere without a license from the Board of Trade; and the Town and Country Planning Act, which gave the government power to take over whole areas for the building of new towns by specially established public corporations.[29] While all these powers for long-range location of industry were used to some extent, it is claimed by some observers that this planning was at best piecemeal and uncoordinated. All geographical planning was allegedly conducted in a "restricted frame of reference." [30] Dr. Brady argues that there was "no evidence at all of the existence of any such national plan" for the location of industry.[31] Clearly, however, there were detailed plans for industrial location within specific areas.

---

[29] Williams, *op. cit.*, p. 93.

[30] Brady, *op. cit.*, pp. 650–651.

[31] *Ibid.*, p. 651.

On balance, the picture of economic planning in the United Kingdom under the Labor government is blurred. No doubt, most socialist supporters of the Labor Party were dissatisfied with the absence or looseness of the degree of planning that was attained by the time the party was voted out of office in 1951. Many of them also had misgivings about the limited goal for planning that the Laborites ultimately set for themselves. Planning is an alluring concept—at least in prospect. It is extremely difficult to realize, as the Soviet leaders learned before the Labor Party.

The British concept of planning is far different from the Soviet. Whereas the Soviet Union is committed to detailed production plans, rigidly supervised and enforced by the government, in the United Kingdom the Labor government aimed for a framework of consistent targets that would influence public officials and private business. It wanted to make control over private industry primarily voluntary. (Presumably, if industry would not accept what it considered reasonable compromises, the Labor government would use coercion.)

The Labor Party could hope to maintain full employment largely through control over government investment. This control it had facilitated by the fact that many basic industries had been nationalized. Its long range plans for the location of industry apparently were only partial in scope; coordination of regional plans on a national level was lacking. A major economic control under the Labor government was the allocation of raw materials, which is a general as well as a specific form of control. Nevertheless, the machinery for national and general economic planning was created under the Labor government. Perhaps when sufficient skilled personnel became available to make it possible, the Labor government would have expanded its range of planning activities significantly. However, as one journal put it, there was a "trend away from planning, even among the Labor planners." [32]

C] NATIONALIZATION OF INDUSTRY IN THE UNITED KINGDOM

The Labor government emphatically did not propose to nationalize all industry, even though it stated: "Its ultimate purpose at home is the establishment of the Socialist Commonwealth of Great Britain . . .".[33] Its nationalization goal was set at between

---

[32] *Business Week,* March 18, 1950, p. 60.

[33] "Let Us Face the Future," Sec. IV.

20 and 30 per cent of all industry for the immediate future. The industries it nationalized included the Bank of England, coal, gas, transport (including rail, inland shipping, and trucking), electricity, civil aviation, and overseas cable communication.[34] Projected for nationalization by the Labor Party are cement, beet sugar manufacture, sugar refining, and sections of the chemical industry;[35] however, further nationalization had been postponed temporarily in 1950. "The nationalized sector of the British economy will . . . always remain a minority of the whole. Total national ownership of all the means of production and distribution once advocated in most early socialist doctrines does not come within the modern socialist concept as it exists in Britain." [36]

Nationalization of industry is not exclusively the idea of the British Labor Government. The Conservatives endorse, though perhaps not wholeheartedly, nationalization of most of the currently nationalized industries. At the time they objected to the nationalization of transport, electricity, and gas—and most vigorously to iron and steel.

1. *Motives for Nationalization*

While it seems that the enthusiasm for nationalization among all groups in the Labor Party has been waning in recent years, nationalization remains nevertheless a major plank of the party platform for several reasons:

First, it gives the government an opportunity to remedy defects in an industry without being hindered by the potentially conflicting interests of private owners. Second, nationalization is politically necessary to insure the continued support of the doctrinaire socialists in the Labor Party. Third, nationalization will facilitate economic planning. Control over the basic industries gives power to control the industries dependent upon them for supplies. The output of most products and services can be restricted, for example, by limiting the amount of steel, coal, electric power, and transportation available for their production. Fourth, and closely related to the first, nationalization is partly intended to prevent interference with the government's economic program. One major figure in the Labor government described the reason for nationalizing the steel

[34] The iron and steel industries were denationalized in 1952.

[35] "Let Us Win Through Together."

[36] Williams, *op. cit.*, p. 91.

industry in the following terms: "If it remains in the hands of its present owners, it will always be possible for them to prevent the effective working of any national economic plan if they so desire."[37]

A fifth reason for nationalizing the major industries is to facilitate a program of employment stabilization. The nationalized industries are intended to play an important part in correcting a slump. They all require large-scale development programs if they are to be effectively modernized and brought up to date. "Should a slump begin to develop, then these vast reconstruction programmes could definitely be speeded up." [38]

2. *Characteristics of Nationalization Measures*

While there are significant differences among the individual nationalization measures, they have the following characteristics in common: First, they all provide for compensation of private owners at approximately the current value of the investment. There have been two principles of compensation applied. One aimed at giving the owners the same income they had been getting under private ownership. In the coal and Bank of England cases, this principle was applied. In most of the other cases, the aim was to give the owners securities whose capital value was equal to the market value of their stock prior to nationalization.

Second, all nationalization measures have established "public corporations" to administer the industry. The running of the nationalized industries in England is not, contrary to common opinion, entrusted to the workers or their representatives. (Recall that the Soviet Union proclaims itself to be a "Workers' State"; its industries are therefore asserted to be under the direction of workers' representatives.) In the United Kingdom, laborers in nationalized industries have only advisory powers in addition to the power they exercise through their unions. Management of nationalized industries often includes persons who had previously been private owners or managers. Technically, legally, and in substance, the nationalized industries are "controlled" by the government. The government, in turn, is responsible to a variety of economic interests, including private owners (of other industries), the middle classes, professionals, farmers and farm laborers, as well as industrial workers. The importance of this point cannot be overemphasized. Workers

---

[37] John Parker, *Labour Marches On* (London: Penguin Books, Ltd., 1947), p. 65.
[38] *Ibid.*, p. 57.

in nationalized industries do not—nor is it clear that they should—regard themselves as bargaining with representatives of all labor.

Third, the administration of nationalized industries is highly centralized. In almost every case, autonomous boards are given full responsibility for the operations of the industry, subject only to the review of Parliament. As a matter of strong tradition, Parliament leaves boards in charge of public corporations very much alone. Councils representing consumers and labor are established, but they possess only advisory powers. The boards must bargain with representatives of the labor union. Unions are explicitly granted the right to strike in nationalized industries.

Fourth, nationalized industries are run with close reference to costs and revenues—much like any privately run corporation. Each nationalized industry is required to pay its way over a period of years.[39] At any given time, however, a minister could decide to run the industry at a loss. The Labor Party has made it clear that it does not consider the meeting of expenses a necessary criterion of success under all circumstances. In the absence of special circumstances—such as a depression, the desire to subsidize the consumption of a particular service, and the like, however, the government does want nationalized industries to meet the tests of efficiency that must be met by private enterprise. (Of course, to the extent that nationalized industries could ordinarily meet costs by raising rates—since they are monopolies within their field—they could cover costs and still be inefficient.)

Fifth, in every case, except possibly in the case of the gas and the iron and steel industries, about which there would be some dispute, the Labor government nationalized industries whose productive performance had been admittedly defective, and in which private owners made only meager profits. In its plans for future nationalization, however, it concentrated upon the existence of antisocial restrictive practices and monopoly.[40] Industries nationalized suffered from one or more of the following: insufficient investment, lack of coordination, inadequate services, and a low level of productive efficiency.

[39] Nationalization Reports, British Information Services, I.D. 1018, June, 1950, p. 2.

[40] "Let Us Win through Together," section entitled "Encouragement for Enterprise."

3. *Results of Nationalization*

Most of the intended results of nationalization could not have been achieved in the short time since the nationalization program has been under way. Not only has the period been short; it has been one in which the special advantages of nationalization could not be enjoyed due to the balance of trade difficulties and domestic shortages that plagued the British economy from the time the Labor Party took power. In addition, the government had no occasion to use the nationalized industries as a major instrument in stabilizing employment.

Criteria have been advanced[41] which, if used in combination and applied carefully, help to indicate the success of nationalization. These include: (1) operating results—changes in output and productivity; (2) financial results—net profits or losses, after noting changes in prices charged; (3) development progress—pace of reorganization and re-equipment; (4) human relations in the industry—number of labor disputes and the sense of "true participation" on the part of the workers. By these tests, the experience of the United Kingdom with nationalization has been neither spectacularly good nor bad. For the most part, total output and productivity in nationalized industries have risen. Whether they would have increased more or less under private ownership can only be conjectured. Labor disputes in nationalized industries, after a choppy beginning, have fallen off and are now low by absolute and relative standards. Some of the nationalized industries were still incurring financial deficits in 1951 (specifically, coal and civil aviation).

Any assessment of nationalization on the basis of British experience thus far would be hasty. The period has been brief and abnormal, and the results so far have not been very strikingly favorable or unfavorable. It will take much more time to tell.

D] IMPROVEMENTS IN PRODUCTIVE EFFICIENCY

Most of British industry is privately owned. If British output is to be increased substantially, private industry must be made more efficient. Inasmuch as many British industries are relatively inefficient, it is a major task of any British government to increase

[41] "Nationalization Reports," British Information Services, I.D. 1018, June, 1950. These criteria have also been applied to the major nationalized industries in this brief report.

productivity. The Labor government was not willing to wait for private industry to modernize its plant and equipment as it chose. Instead, it developed an active program whereby the government could assist and prod private industry to modernize and improve its productive methods. The two major elements of the government program to increase productive efficiency include Working Parties and subsidized industrial research.

1. *The Working Parties*

Working Parties are committees created to investigate various proposals for improvements of organization, production, and distribution methods and processes, and to suggest measures to make industry more stable and more capable of meeting foreign competition.[42] Working Parties are composed of approximately equal numbers of employers, trade unionists, and independent specialists (that is, engineers, economists, management experts, and the like). The recommendations of these parties are purely advisory both to the government and to private industrialists. Up to 1949, the British Board of Trade, which is in charge of most of the Working Party Program, established seventeen Working Parties.

The power of these parties is insignificant from the legal point of view. However, an industry that fails to carry out the major recommendations of the Working Party exposes itself to a demand for nationalization on grounds of technological backwardness and uncooperativeness.

The reports of the Working Parties have varied in detail and insight. All of them, however, have made amply clear that British industry is far less efficient than is possible in the current state of technology. Among the major causes for Britain's technical backwardness (that is, backwardness in the kinds of equipment in use, not in the caliber of the best equipment that is produced mostly for export) are the following: first, British industry is relatively small scale; second, vertical integration is less common than in the United States; third, standardization of output, making possible interchangeable parts, is not practiced as much as practicable; fourth, expenditures for industrial research have been small.[43]

The Working Parties have brought first-rate brains to bear on the problem of technical efficiency. Businessmen who may have

[42] Brady, *op. cit.*, pp. 531–532.

[43] Based largely on Brady, *op. cit.*, pp. 9, 641–653.

been inefficient due to a lack of understanding about what might be done now know how they could increase productivity. The Working Parties have, in this way, performed a vital service. Whether their recommendations will be followed soon and extensively enough to substantially improve productive efficiency cannot yet be judged. Legislation has been enacted known as the Industrial Organization and Development Act for the establishment of Development Councils, composed of representatives of private owners, labor, and government to achieve the objectives and to carry out the program recommended by Working Parties.[44] This measure was enacted over the strong opposition of industry.

2. *Subsidization of Industrial Research*

At a time when the Soviet Union was spending about 1 per cent of its national income for research, and the United States was spending about 0.5 per cent, a cabinet minister estimated that the United Kingdom was spending 0.1 per cent on a per capita basis.[45] To no small degree, the technical backwardness of the United Kingdom is attributable to this cause. Perhaps in larger measure, the trouble is with the understanding and use of science, which in turn results from a lack of trained men to apply scientific discoveries to industrial use.[46] Professor Brady thinks the major obstacles to technical efficiency are the "indifference, even resistance, shown by both government and industry to the adoption of new techniques, and the failure to comprehend the requirements and implications of mass production methods." [47]

Considerable effort has been made to increase industrial research. The war itself stimulated private research activity, and the government has taken a variety of measures to increase it further. There have been established an advisory Council on Scientific Policy and a Committee on Industrial Productivity, both charged with promoting and coordinating scientific work in the United King-

---

[44] The relation between Working Parties and Development Councils is not altogether clear. Development Councils can do all that the Working Parties are expected to do and more.

[45] These figures were presented by Sir Harold Hartly in 1943. Their precise meaning is vague in the extreme. Quoted by Brady, *op. cit.*, p. 643, from D. W. Hill, *Co-operative Research in Industry* (London: Hutchinson & Co., Ltd., 1946).

[46] This view was expressed by the Lord President in reviewing the first report of the Advisory Council on Scientific Policy. See Brady, *op. cit.*, p. 645.

[47] *Ibid.*

dom; the Department for Scientific and Industrial Research was empowered to substantially subsidize industrial research. Interest in industrial research is running high and the Labor government clearly stimulated research activity. It is still too early to tell to what extent laboratory findings will be put to use.

E] OTHER MAJOR ELEMENTS IN THE LABOR GOVERNMENT'S ECONOMIC PROGRAM

Although the major components of the Labor government's program have been described, some fairly important measures have not been mentioned, particularly the program for agriculture, the antimonopoly program, the "utility schemes," and controls over foreign trade.

1. *The Program for Agriculture*

The government, through the Ministry of Food, now buys the greater part of British farm output either directly or through authorized agents. It then resells these products to consumers through various channels. By means of centralized buying, the government exerts great influence over the pattern of agriculture. It establishes guaranteed prices eighteen months in advance to enable farmers to plan ahead, to permit farmers to pay wages high enough to attract new workers to agriculture, and to stimulate the output of desired crops. In addition, centralized buying permits the government to carry out a policy of subsidization of desired types of food consumption with facility.[48]

2. *The Antimonopoly Program*

Another major plank of the Labor government's long-range program was the elimination of antisocial monopolistic practices. Considerable fanfare surrounded the discussion and adoption of an antimonopoly law in 1948. The Labor Party has frequently charged that monopoly (more specifically, participation by British firms in international cartels) is the cause of important weaknesses in the British economy.

The antimonopoly legislation adopted by the United Kingdom differs in method but not in objective from the American antitrust laws. In the three years following their adoption, the British antimonopoly laws produced virtually no results. More precisely,

---

[48] Williams, *op. cit.*, p. 98.

the Monopoly Commission established by the Act produced two reports during this period dealing with two minor industries that together employ only 9,000 workers. All parties supported a resolution in Parliament that called for a speeding up of the work of the Monopoly Commission.[49]

3. *The "Utility Schemes"*

A wide variety of consumers' goods in Britain are produced according to standards established by the government in consultation with private industry. These goods are free from the purchase tax, which must be paid on similar goods produced outside the utility program, and are designed with particular care for durability and serviceability. Roughly 40 per cent of the nonutility price is saved by those who purchase utility goods. Utility goods cover a wide range of products, including cotton, rayon, linen, and wool cloth; apparel; footwear; household textiles; furniture; and bedding. Utility goods are subject to strict price controls (which apply also to over a third of total personal consumption expenditure). The purpose of the utility schemes is to insure a supply of important types of consumer goods in the home market at reasonable prices. Control over the quality of these products, moreover, protects the consumer against a waste of income through uninformed purchasing at a time when austerity is unavoidable. The utility schemes also contribute toward increased standardization of output and may yield cost benefits and help overcome the excessive individuality of output in many spheres.

4. *Controls over Foreign Trade*

The import of major foodstuffs and raw materials is controlled by an elaborate system of import licensing. Some imports are purchased abroad by centralized purchasing agencies, namely, cotton, copper, lead, zinc, aluminum, jute, sulfur, pyrites, mining timber, plywood, and soft woods. When acquired by the government, some of these products are allocated among users according to some general plan. The government also fixes the prices for these products. Restrictions have been placed on the quantities of certain products that may be imported. However, there are now no restrictions on im-

---

[49] For the interesting debate over this resolution, which consists largely of an evaluation of progress made thus far, see Hansard, *Parliamentary Debates*, June 15, 1951, col. 2697–2796.

ports from countries whose currency is not scarce in the United Kingdom ("soft currency" countries).

Export controls were also imposed by the Labor government, though few of these are compulsory in nature. Some goods are reserved exclusively for export. Most exports, however, are influenced by exhortation, voluntary agreement, and by agreements under which domestic producers receive allocations of raw materials.

F] CONCLUSIONS ABOUT THE LABOR GOVERNMENT'S ECONOMIC PROGRAM

The picture of British economy that emerges from the foregoing analysis of its major component parts may be summarized in the following general conclusions:

1. The government, by nationalization, direct regulation, subsidy, encouragement, example, and voluntary agreement with businessmen, helps to decide many matters that are determined by independent businessmen in the United States.

2. In the United Kingdom, the monetary incentives for workers are relatively weak—perhaps weaker than in the Soviet Union. Tax rates are very high and the penalties for inefficiency and for not working are diluted by the provisions for social security legislation. Businessmen are partly influenced by negative incentives—in the form of veiled threats of nationalization.

3. The economy is not carefully coordinated either by powerful planning machinery or by a freely working price system.

IV. HOW THE BASIC ECONOMIC PROBLEMS ARE "SOLVED" IN THE UNITED KINGDOM

Most of the discussion of the economies of the United States and the Soviet Union was organized around the following questions: Who decides what shall be produced and by what methods? How are individuals directed into their occupations? How is income distributed? How progressive is the economy? The discussion of the United Kingdom thus far has singled out its novel features. While most of the questions raised about the United States and the Soviet Union can probably be answered for Great Britain on the basis of what has already been said, those questions will be briefly considered.

A] WHO DECIDES WHAT SHALL BE PRODUCED IN THE UNITED KINGDOM?

As in the United States and the Soviet Union, the consumer in the United Kingdom is free to buy almost everything he can pay for. However, the range of choice open to the consumer is limited in a variety of ways. Government actions that influence the choices made by the consumer include primarily the following.

First, a fairly long list of items are rationed. Most important among the products rationed at the beginning of 1951 were meat, bacon, cheese, butter, margarine, cooking fats, tea, sugar, chocolate, sugar confectionery, and animal feeding stuffs.[50] This rationing system limits consumers' freedom of choice by restricting the amount and the proportion in which they purchase individual consumers' goods.

Second, the government influences the output of a long list of consumers' goods whose production requires basic materials like steel and lumber. It exerts this influence by the manner in which it allocates the supplies of these basic materials. Closely related to the effect of allocations of raw materials upon output are the various devices, already described, by which the government determines the proportion of the national income to be invested and the proportion to be used for producing consumers' goods.

Third, by its price controls and particularly its large subsidy program for food, the government strongly influences the consumption and production of many vital consumers' goods. These controls do not infringe upon consumers' freedom to purchase whatever they choose of unrationed goods. However, they substantially alter the character of the choices the consumer can make and thereby they profoundly affect the decisions he does make. There really is not much difference between directly increasing the supply of, say, potatoes by 30 per cent and so rearranging the prices of potatoes and their substitutes that people do produce and purchase 30 per cent more.

Fourth, the government influences the available supply of many, if not most, imported products through its foreign exchange controls. By means of these controls, government representatives decide who, among those desiring to import goods from abroad, is to be permitted to do so.

---

[50] "Controls in the United Kingdom," distributed by the British Information Services, January 24, 1951, p. 4.

Fifth, by cooperating in the setting down of quality specifications and in freeing some goods from heavy purchase taxes through its "utility schemes," the government strongly influences consumers' choices. In this case, the government increases the range of choices open to consumers and leaves them free to choose what they wish. Strong price inducements are offered for the purchase of utility goods.

As in any country, there are many and subtle influences upon the choices of British consumers. Social pressure and "class" consumption patterns are said to be stronger influences on British consumers' choices than on American consumers. Because of the greater rigidity of social classes in the United Kingdom than in the United States, the attempts to emulate the consumption patterns of the most prosperous classes is probably less common there than here. Advertising, less widely employed in the United Kingdom than in the United States, is used more frequently than it is in the Soviet Union. It differs in quantity from American advertising, but it is less compulsive and more informative. While it doubtless influences consumers' choices—that is its obvious motive—it seems to have far less influence than American advertising. (It should be stressed that the difference between British and American advertising is in no way due to actions taken by the Labor government.)

The Labor Party, in its 1950 election manifesto,[51] promised to establish Consumers' Advisory Centers to advise consumers on the relative merits of available goods. It had not carried out this promise by the time it was voted out of office. The intention of this proposal is to influence strongly though indirectly the choices consumers make and the kinds of goods offered to them.

B] DETERMINATION OF THE METHODS OF PRODUCTION TO BE EMPLOYED

We want to know, among other things, whether the persons who decide what methods of production are to be used are employees of the government or of privately owned firms; how great is their knowledge about production techniques; and whether they are strongly motivated in the direction of minimizing real costs. Most methods of doing business in the United Kingdom are selected by independent owners of private businesses. As indicated, in many industries the government assists them (by means of Working Party

51 "Let Us Win Through Together."

reports and Development Councils) to discover methods of becoming more efficient. In part, also, the government puts pressure on them to employ efficient methods of production by a veiled threat of nationalization. (Of course, we do not really know how likely the government is to nationalize backward industries or how seriously the private businessmen take the threat.)

The government directly determines production methods in the industries that have been nationalized. However, current production techniques reflect past decisions of private owners; they have been modified only slightly in the short period since nationalization went into effect. Also, in its extensive program to stimulate industrial research, the government also affects the methods of production used in both privately and publicly owned industry. While the government unquestionably exerts considerable influence over methods of production in the United Kingdom, they are still determined in the main by private businessmen.

C] THE ALLOCATION OF INDIVIDUALS AMONG OCCUPATIONS

British subjects are free to enter whatever occupations they choose subject to licensing and educational restrictions in some trades and to union restrictions in others. (Up to 1950, the British government held and used, although sparingly, the power to direct labor into particular occupations. This power, however, was allowed to lapse.)

In two particulars the United Kingdom differs from the United States somewhat in the conditions that determine the occupations that individuals enter. First, free tuition for advanced education is available to a larger proportion of the best students there than here. The government also pays for the maintenance of some students during their training periods, as is done in the Soviet Union.[52] Second, the British government labor exchanges (employment services) are much more efficient and are used much more by employers than is the case in the United States. (Among other differences, the British employment exchanges are national in scope.) Accordingly, British workers are better informed than American workers about

---

[52] Nearly 70 per cent of British university students are receiving financial assistance from other than private sources. Of the expenditures by the Ministry of Education for advanced training between April, 1945, and January, 1950, £30.6 million went for maintenance and £8.6 million for tuition fees.—*Britain 1950–51*, pp. 232 and 233.

available job opportunities. Those two differences do not alter significantly the fundamental similarity between the United States and the United Kingdom in the manner that individuals' occupations are determined.

D] THE DISTRIBUTION OF PERSONAL INCOME

Differences in personal income in the United Kingdom are very substantial—before income taxes are paid. After taxes, as already indicated, personal income in the United Kingdom is distributed far more equally than in the United States.

Apart from the greater redistribution of income by means of personal taxes and welfare expenditure, income distribution differs from ours for several reasons: First, British agriculture is much more prosperous than ours; here agriculture is the chief source of low incomes (save during depression, when unemployed industrial workers are the lowest income recipients). Second, public provision of vital services that must be purchased privately in the United States contributes toward greater equality of real income in the United Kingdom; most important of these services is free medical care, which assures the poorest Englishman of an essential that most American poor lack. Finally, all but very small families in England are helped by children's allowances, which grant 15 shillings weekly (the equivalent of about $1.75) for each child after the first.

As in the United States, and in sharp contrast to the Soviet Union, the largest British personal incomes are obtained primarily from property. Past huge inequalities in personal fortunes are therefore still resulting in current income inequalities. However, the British income tax levies substantially higher rates of tax on income from property than on income from wages and salaries; because of this form of tax, the relationship between property distribution and income distribution has been blunted.

The part of British economic experience that probably interests Americans most is the effect of high taxes upon productive incentive. As indicated, one investigator could find no adverse effect on total output or productivity, and himself concluded that it did not damage entrepreneurial incentive.[53] However, in interpreting these conclusions, one should recognize that the effect of taxation on incentives cannot be estimated accurately. One might, as Mr. Weaver did, compare changes in production and productivity in the United

[53] Weaver, *op. cit.*, p. 201.

Kingdom with similar conditions in other countries. (He compared Great Britain with the United States.) While very revealing, such a comparison is not the same as comparing what happened with what would have happened if taxes had been lower.

High tax rates in the United Kingdom clearly have not "killed" incentive. Incentives may have been dampened, however. In the author's opinion, taxation in the United Kingdom has gone farther than desirable for a nation that is so anxious to expand output and to raise productivity. For example, income taxes in 1951 on incomes over the equivalent of $42,500 took 97.5 per cent of all additional income.[54] High taxes on corporate profits probably encouraged large firms to pursue a conservative investment policy.

It is recognized that high tax rates probably contributed greatly to the high morale of the poor. Possibly without such high taxes on incomes and corporate profits general social unrest would have been far greater.

E] THE PROGRESSIVENESS OF THE BRITISH ECONOMY

Little can be added to what has already been said about the influences at work on technological advance. The government participates actively in stimulating industrial research. Moreover, it has fostered the creation of Working Parties and Development Councils that bring representatives of owners, labor, and government together to improve production technique and product design.

It is far too early to say whether the British economy will become as progressive as, say, the American economy. There can be little doubt, however, that it now has greater opportunities and pressure for progress; substantial improvement over past performance can therefore be anticipated, despite the high tax rates.

Now that the major characteristics of the British economy have been described, an attempt will be made to assess the achievements of the British Labor government on balance.

V. ACCOMPLISHMENTS OF THE UNITED KINGDOM UNDER THE LABOR GOVERNMENT

As indicated in connection with the evaluation of the economy of the Soviet Union, it is impossible to formulate reliable standards for the assessment of an economy. The greatest difficulty arises from

[54] *Nation*, December 1, 1951, p. 468.

deciding how much could have been accomplished by alternative means under similar circumstances. Also, it is impossible to decide what value to place on the creation of new arrangements that might improve the operations of the economy in the future. The following general tests are suggested for evaluating an economy that has had too short a history to be judged by the facts. First, to what extent do authorities think the government was successful? Second, what is the judgment of the electorate? Third, what actually happened to output and productivity? The best possible judgment will be made by using all three tests in combination. These tests will be applied to the British economy.

A] EVALUATION OF EXPERTS

Relatively few exhaustive and impartial analyses of the British economy have been made. Textbook discussions of the economy under the Labor government have been generally sympathetic, but have ordinarily ended on the note that "we must wait and see." [55] The analysis of the Labor government's program prepared by Professor Brady, perhaps the most exhaustive, is quite critical. Paradoxically, he criticizes the Laborites for planning too little, while most critics take the position that they plan too much.

The criticism most frequently made by competent and impartial critics of the Labor government is that it did not make adequate use of the price system but, instead, relied excessively upon direct controls. Even some intellectual socialists feel that the Labor Party leaders naïvely assumed that controls were always to be preferred to no controls.

To take one case in point, Professor Meade would have removed rent controls in order to encourage people to economize in the use of space, to allow those whose need for living quarters was most urgent to bid them away from persons needing them less, and to increase private incentives to increase living space. However, in conjunction with a removal of rent controls, he would impose "a temporary and diminishing tax on the occupation of dwellings which would ensure that the difference between the new and the old rents paid by tenants accrued to the State and not to the landlords."

---

[55] See W. N. Loucks and J. W. Hoot, *Comparative Economic Systems* (New York: Harper & Brothers, 1948), pp. 357–449; R. Blodgett, *Comparative Economic Systems* (New York: The Macmillan Company, rev. ed., 1949); G. N. Halm, *Economic Systems* (New York: Rinehart & Company, Inc., 1951), pp. 361–387; and Sikes, *op. cit.*, pp. 142–202.

Moreover, he would try to meet any hardships involved in such an arrangement by higher family allowances and old-age pensions.[56] He thus concedes that considerable interference with wholly uncontrolled rents was required under the circumstances, and simply disagrees about the particular controls that were chosen. None of the responsible critics of the Labor government would have advocated thorough abandonment of all controls; each had his particular objection. All together they represent an expression of greater faith in the price system than was exhibited by the Labor government.

Most discussions of the Labor government's program are partisan. Many have been written by members of the Labor Party, while a large number have been written by economists opposed to government control on principle. Marxists and left-wing socialists have also written about the Labor government's performance. As might have been expected, the first group is laudatory, the other two are critical. Only the direct supporters of the Labor government feel that it found just the right degree of interference with private business. Others criticize it for "planning" too much or too little.

Thus, there is no clear consensus of opinion among authorities about the Labor government's performance. The assorted views help to evaluate the Laborite program only by ruling out the possibility that it has been either an unqualified success or an unmitigated failure.

B] THE ELECTORATE'S EVALUATION OF THE LABOR GOVERNMENT

The results of the 1950 and 1951 elections, the only ones held since Labor came to power, neither repudiate nor endorse the Labor Party. Indeed, they show very little change in the popularity of the party since 1945.

The following table indicates the number of popular votes obtained by the three major parties in the United Kingdom in 1945, 1950, and 1951, and the number of seats they held in Parliament. As indicated in that table, Labor's vote increased in each election. Indeed, Labor obtained a larger proportion of the popular vote in 1951, when it received 48.8 per cent, than it did in 1945 or 1950, when it received 48.2 and 46.3 per cent respectively. The rise in Labor vote apparently resulted from the larger total vote cast, and from the virtual disappearance of the Liberal Party as a factor in British politics.

---

[56] Meade, *op. cit.*, p. ix.

TABLE 4-4

Popular Vote and Parliament Seats of Major British Parties, 1945, 1950, 1951

Year	Popular vote			Seats in Parliament		
	Labor	Conservative	Liberal	Labor	Conservative	Liberal
1945	12,039	9,201	2,245	396	213	12
1950	13,296	12,502	2,621	315	299	9
1951	13,912	13,721	724	294	321	6

SOURCE: *British Record, Political and Economic Notes,* October 31, 1951.

Several points should be considered in interpreting these results, which seem to show neither hearty approval nor strong disapproval. First, the British press is heavily weighted against the Labor Party. Over the nationalized broadcasting system, the Labor government got at least an even break, however.

Second, the election of 1945 cannot be construed as support for the Labor Party's program as much as a vote in opposition to the "old way of doing things." The specific content of the Labor Party's program apparently did not alienate many persons who supported it in protest. On the other hand, it did not gain many new supporters after 1945 either. If its program had been a substantial success in the eyes of the electorate, its majorities would have grown.

Third, the period during which the Laborites ruled prior to the 1950 election was one of economic hardship, during which living standards were below wartime levels. Voters typically turn an incumbent party out of office under such circumstances, even if it is not responsible for the difficulties.

Fourth, some British citizens were led to believe that economic help from the United States would not be continued if they were to re-elect the Labor government. Many United States Congressmen made it clear that their opposition to aiding the United Kingdom was due to the fact that Britain was "socialist." The very narrow vote by which the British loan of 1946 and Marshall Plan Aid were authorized may have induced some persons who otherwise would have voted Labor to give their vote to the Conservatives. On the other hand, many Britons may have been enraged at the implication that the United States would interfere in domestic British affairs and may even have shifted their vote to support the Labor Party. On balance, it would seem that the Conservatives received some support from those who expected American economic assistance to be greater if the Conservatives were elected.

Given the stability of the proportion of the popular vote received by the Labor government, and in view of the factors that might lead one to expect a decline in public support even if the government had done a reasonably effective job, the performance of the Labor government is unclear if judged by the response of the voters. By this test too it is neither a success nor a failure.

C] CHANGES IN OUTPUT AND PRODUCTIVITY UNDER THE LABOR GOVERNMENT

We can use "synthetic" statistics to measure the output of British industry, for we know how they are computed and we know that the methods used are generally acceptable. The government prepares indexes of all mining and manufacturing output, and for manufacturing output alone, and agricultural production. Together they describe changes in total British output quite fully. As Table 4-5 indicates, output has grown substantially in the United Kingdom since the end of World War II, having risen by about 35 to 40 per cent over all. Compared with the 1938 output, 1950 industrial production in the United Kingdom was up by about 35 per cent.[57]

TABLE 4-5

Postwar Output in the United Kingdom

Output	1946	1947	1948	1949	1950
Industrial production	100	108	121	129	140
Manufacturing output	100	109	123	132	145
Total net agricultural output (as % of 1936–1939)	. . .	122*	134*	139*	

* The agricultural output is reported for crop years, which overlap calendar years.

SOURCE: *Economic Survey for 1951,* Command 8195, April, 1951, pp. 18, 25.

Perhaps more revealing of economic progress than total output are data describing productivity—that is, the average output of each

[57] See *Monthly Bulletin of Statistics,* prepared by the Statistical Office of the United Nations.

worker. By this measure also, the United Kingdom under the Labor government achieved substantial progress. For example, while industrial production between 1946 and 1950 increased 40 per cent, employment rose only 15 per cent. Thus, the average rise in productivity amounted to about 22 per cent in a three-year period. As Table 4-6 shows, the rate of increase was greater between 1949 and 1950 than it was between 1948 and 1949. An even greater increase in productivity took place in manufacturing industry. The maintenance of the large rate of productivity increase into 1950 was not even anticipated by the Labor government.[58]

TABLE 4-6

Labor Productivity in Industry and in Manufacturing

Industrial production	*1947*	*1948*	*1949*	*1950*	*1951*
Output	108	121	129	140	144
Employment	108	111	112	115	117
Productivity (index)	100	109	115	122	123
Manufacturing industries					
Output	109	123	132	145	
Employment	107	110	112	115	
Productivity (index)	102	112	118	126	

SOURCE: *Economic Survey for 1951,* Command 8195, April, 1951, p. 18; for 1951, *Britain in Brief* (British Information Services, December, 1952), p. 2.

Some economists assert that total output and productivity data of the type here presented are misleading. They contend that the United Kingdom is producing the wrong things and that actually the value of what is being produced is declining rather than increasing. The strongest exponent of this position is Dr. John Jewkes, a British economist, whose views are endorsed by several other economists. In effect, he contends that the regulations imposed by the Labor government have so distorted the economy that measurements of output have lost most of their meaning. He writes: "The net output of finished goods from the labor and raw materials available was much lower than it would have been in a free market purged of the inflationary pressure. . . . The vicious circle was complete. In-

[58] *Economic Survey for 1951,* Command 8195, April, 1951, p. 18.

flation unattended to; controls over the distribution of resources to prevent price rises; *maldistribution of resources because of the inherent clumsiness of controls;* dwindling production intensifying the inflation; more controls and so on, endlessly." [59] Dr. Halm says: "This account of planning and control in Britain is hardly too extreme . . ." [60]

It is not clear how Dr. Jewkes can tell whether and how much the allocation of resources was worsened by the government. It is far from clear that another government would have been more successful in combating inflation; moreover, a "free market," even if not "purged of inflationary pressure," could hardly be anticipated, no matter what government took power.

There can be no question that the kinds of goods produced in the United Kingdom today differ from those that would have been produced in the absence of the Labor government's many controls. However, it is debatable whether the present composition of output is either better or worse than it would have been under another government. This author believes that the data on output and productivity presented are fairly reliable indicators of the success of the Labor government's economic program.

D] NONECONOMIC EFFECTS OF THE LABOR GOVERNMENT'S PROGRAM

It is difficult to determine what, if any, noneconomic effects the Labor government's program has had. Any changes in personal attitudes, psychological states, social conditions, and political arrangements since 1945 could far more easily be attributed to World War II, the cold war, and the threat of another war than to changes brought about by the government. One might also expect to find changes, however, that have not yet appeared.

Possibly the average British subject already is less worried about the likelihood of prolonged unemployment during his lifetime than he was before 1945. However, one cannot tell whether the average British citizen is confident that the government will be able to maintain full employment. The consensus of opinion seems to be that the fear of unemployment is smaller than before, but still is

[59] John Jewkes, *Ordeal by Planning* (New York: The Macmillan Company, 1948), p. 77. (The italics are the author's.)

[60] Halm, *op. cit.*, p. 372.

not small. Similarly, the British surely feel far more secure against impoverishment due to sickness than before. However, one cannot tell how much their personal happiness has increased as a result.

Perhaps the most important noneconomic issue that should be raised about the Labor government's program is its effect on political democracy. Some people contend that extensive economic activities on the part of government inevitably weaken the control of the average citizen over the government.[61] This thesis runs as follows: When government regulates business in many ways, it becomes the major giver of "favors" in all forms. The government will keep itself in power by "buying off" any group that seems able to prevent its continuation in office by giving it favors. Also, intimidation and discriminatory treatment will be employed by the government against those who oppose it.

The argument that extensive government controls mean the weakening, if not the end, of democracy may turn out to be correct in the future. Up to the present, no weakening in the quality of democracy in the United Kingdom is visible. Some students assert on the contrary that there was greater interest and participation in government under the Labor government than there was before,[62] because people are influenced by government's actions to a larger extent. They also see no evidence that the Labor Party was insincere when it pledged itself to protect democracy, if necessary, at the expense of socialism. Certainly an undemocratic government would not have permitted itself to be voted out of power without making more strenuous use of its economic controls than was made by the Labor Party in 1951.

There is some fear that the greater equality of income in the United Kingdom and the spread of equalitarian attitudes associated with it is likely to result in a leveling down to mediocrity. The cultured and cultivated product of the wealthy classes provided the nation's political, business, and intellectual leaders. There is some anxiety lest no substitute leaders or only leaders of lesser caliber will be available hereafter.

---

[61] The most widely discussed presentation of this thesis is to be found in F. A. Hayek, *The Road to Serfdom* (Chicago: University of Chicago Press, 1944).

[62] University of Chicago Round Table, *The British Welfare State: What Is It?* discussion by Mark Abrams, Edward Shils, and Alan Simpson, August 28, 1949, especially pp. 7-9.

Workers and farmers achieved a new and high status under the Labor government. Persons from their ranks were given the highest offices and made members of the nobility. They may feel that their importance is for the first time recognized by society in general and from this feeling they doubtless take considerable satisfaction.

VI. CONCLUSIONS

In a relatively short time, the Labor government substantially altered the British economy. It inaugurated many economic experiments that are likely to yield results of lasting value.

In evaluating the contribution and performance of the Labor government, it would be easy to criticize it for pursuing policies that were politically expedient, though they were not economically correct. But can one expect, and should he even ask, that a political party adopt policies that will drive it from power—especially when its successors would not adopt the necessary policies either? This author believes that the Labor government could have been more resolute on some points without losing public favor—indeed, it probably would have increased its following. One major case in point concerns the coal industry, which is crucial to the British economy. When the opportunity to admit a substantial number of Italian miners arose, the Labor government did not strongly press for their admission.

The Labor Party might also be criticized on other scores. It failed to carry out some important parts of its program. Specifically, the antimonopoly program was permitted to languish after a bill was enacted. Too, the Consumers' Advisory Centers were never even established. Moreover, relatively little pressure was put behind the Development Councils and Working Parties. Not a great deal has come of their recommendations.

Finally, this author shares the view of many critics that the Labor government underestimated the use that could be made of the price system. In fairness, however, it should be observed that some of these critics would erect a large body of controls in place of those now existing in order to gain the benefits of the price system's workings. Some of the measures recommended seem administratively unfeasible and politically unacceptable.

Taking its virtues and faults together, the Labor government is best regarded as a peaceful and democratic revolt against the notion that economic systems can run themselves successfully. Its supporters believe that by considerable regulation and control the performance of an economy can be improved. The record of the Labor government, while too short to be conclusive, suggests that this view may be correct for the United Kingdom.

CHAPTER FIVE

Conclusions

The foregoing description of three economies which presented both basic rationale and details of structure and function probably exaggerated the differences among them. They are indeed fundamentally different. However, their important similarities must not be overlooked. Points of similarity in economic systems that are very different in underlying ideology indicate the economic devices that have been proved successful. What are the major points that the American, Soviet, and British economies have in common?

First, it appears that the price system, which is not "pure" or "free" in any of the three systems, is a pillar of all. It seems that regulation of prices by government, business, and labor is on the increase in the United States. In the United Kingdom and the Soviet Union, on the other hand, restrictions on price are being reduced. With the passage of time all three economies seem to be moving closer together in their use of the pricing mechanism.

Second, heavy reliance on monetary incentives is common to all three systems. Inequalities of personal income are substantial in all. However, all of them blunt monetary incentives by progressive taxes upon personal income. Moreover, each treats income from property differently—with less approval or higher taxes—from payments for personal services. The three economies make considerable use of negative incentives. Punishments for not working according to one's employer's directions are strict. None of the three guarantees a decent living to anyone who is unwilling to make considerable productive effort.

Third, the economies of the United States, the Soviet Union, and the United Kingdom are also similar in that they rely heavily upon free choice of occupations and of consumers' goods. Although Soviet and British Labor leaders do not shrink, at least in principle, from using direction or coercion when they think it would help matters substantially, actually they provide relatively free choice to workers and consumers. Freedom in these two matters presumably was found to be efficient in organizing economic activity as well as personally satisfying to the entire population.

Fourth, all three economies have many economic features in common. Money exchange is the rule in all. All resort to both direct and indirect taxes. Banks, exercising borrowing and lending functions, exist in all three. All rely heavily upon specialization and exchange. They employ roundabout methods of production involving high mechanization of production. All require that most of the population work under the direction of others.

Of course, even in the respects in which these economies are fundamentally similar, they differ in degree. It is possible to exaggerate the similarity of the economies of the United States, the Soviet Union, and the United Kingdom. Certainly they are sufficiently different to warrant our considering them different types of economic system.

Apart from the satisfaction of personal curiosity about how other economic systems operate, what conclusions can an American voter draw from the foregoing discussion of the three economies? We must recognize at the outset that an overwhelming majority of Americans is opposed to socialism or communism, or to any other drastic change. Consequently, the question, Should we accept socialism or communism or some other system? is almost completely academic.

The greatest significance to the American voter of the foregoing discussion is its bearing on a central issue around which much popular discussion revolves: Should the government keep its hands off business? Foreign experience in meeting economic problems by employing government controls is definitely relevant to, although not conclusive in, the resolution of our own domestic economic issues. (This discussion made no effort to point up what foreign readers might learn from us; it was written primarily for the American reader.)

No direct and reliable poll of Americans' views has been taken on this issue. Many unquestionably believe that government regulation is bad—no matter what is being regulated and no matter what the circumstances. They might be correct in holding this view, but before a convincing case can be made for it, one must study the effects of all government regulation. The foregoing discussion of the

Soviet Union and the United Kingdom has shown that other major countries regulate, control, and directly operate far more economic processes than we do. As far as it is possible to judge, most people in those countries would not end their government's regulatory activities; many would extend them. These countries—and we ourselves in certain cases—have demonstrated that government regulation sometimes can greatly improve conditions. Or, put differently, at least in the Soviet Union and the United Kingdom, government regulation has not prevented a substantial improvement in economic conditions.

A minority of voters seems to hold a completely opposite view on the question of government control of business. They believe that almost all economic evils can be eliminated and almost anything can be improved simply by passing a law. Experiences in the Soviet Union and in the United Kingdom have shown that many economic processes—notably the choice of jobs and of products—are best left free from regulation.

Clearly, all forms of government regulation cannot simply be assumed to be "bad" or "good." Some kinds of government control fall far short of achieving their goals and give rise to undesirable by-product effects. On the other hand, other kinds improve matters. One can only judge in individual cases whether a particular government regulation will make matters better or worse, or achieve results equal to those of free enterprise. The issue cannot be judged on the basis of general principle alone—that is clear. Only one principle has general validity in a democratic country: all measures, and only those measures, that contribute to general welfare should be adopted.

Clearly, we do not know all there is to know about the way that economic systems behave. We know even less about the methods by which the performance of economic systems might be improved. Tomorrow we may find solutions to problems that we think are insoluble today. We rarely are offered tested and proved remedies. Every new regulation involves the risk of failure, but also might work out better than anticipated. Some risks are involved in any change. If we do not take the risks involved in change, however, we can be *certain* that conditions will not be improved.

The fact that government control may have been effective in another country and in some industries in this country does not prove that more government regulation would be desirable in the United

States. Successful government regulation requires a variety of circumstances that differ widely from country to country and from industry to industry within the same country. For example, big businesses are ordinarily easier to regulate and control than a large number of small ones. Nations with a well-trained civil service with high standards of public service have far better success with government regulation than nations in which government service is not highly regarded. The level of public morality also strongly influences the success with which government regulations achieve their goals. Assistance of the public at large in reporting violations and in assisting the authorities in various ways can spell the difference between government regulations that work well and that work badly. Each regulation that is proposed must be considered in the particular context in which it is to be applied.

For the average American voter, the foregoing discussion of different economic systems has another possible significance. It should increase his tolerance of economic systems that are different from his own. His own economy has been shown to have significant flaws. While other systems may have greater flaws, they still "do make some sense," and have recorded significant achievements in a relatively short time. Accordingly, study of other economics should make the American voter more sympathetic toward and interested in nations that are trying out other types of economic system. In addition, it should indicate that differences in needs, desires, and circumstances from country to country are substantial. No one system is likely to be the best for all nations.

AUTHORS CITED

INDEX

Authors Cited

T

V

W

Index

N

O

P